Better
COOKING
Step-by-step

Elizabeth Pomeroy

Sundial

Contents

First published in 1978 by Sundial Books Limited
59 Grosvenor Street, London W.1.
© Hennerwood Publications Limited
ISBN 0 904230 52 X
Printed in England by Jarrold and Sons Ltd.

Introduction

A happy development of recent years is the growing interest in home cooking. The increasing variety of processed and convenience foods available is counter-balanced by the encouraging number of people who want to cook fresh foods, such as good quality vegetables and fruit and even make their own bread.

Some fortunate people have learned to cook by watching or working with a competent or talented parent, some have been taught cooking at school, but the majority are self-taught. They rely on books, magazines or newspapers for their recipes, on their friends for advice and on their own trials and errors for experience.

This book is designed to help the self-taught cook and adventurous amateur by explaining with pictures the what, why and how of the basic skills of the kitchen — what certain culinary terms mean, why one method is more successful than another and how to make and present many popular dishes.

The book is arranged in sections according to cooking methods. If you long to make a flour-based sauce without lumps, or a creamy sauce which will not curdle, you will find the right method with step-by-step pictures for each one in its own group under Sauces.

If you have had problems frying crisp fish fillets and chips, or roasting poultry, or making a pie, the techniques are explained in the Frying, Roasting and Pastry sections and illustrated with recipes. In this way you can learn the basic skills and how to use them in a variety of ways.

Wise shopping is the first step to successful cooking and guidance on how to choose the right cuts of meat, how to select fresh vegetables and other raw ingredients, is given in the relevant sections.

How to plan and equip the kitchen

In some houses the kitchen is the hub of the home and the centre of family activity, while in a modern flat, because of restricted space, it may be more like a functional workshop. Whether you are planning a friendly spacious kitchen or a kitchenette, both have the same basic necessities — efficient ventilation, adequate plumbing and good lighting.

Ventilation In winter the rising steam and warm air should be able to escape out of the kitchen without letting in cold air. In summer you need to be able to open an ample amount of window to keep the kitchen cool.

A reversible extractor fan will speedily remove steam and cooking smells or suck in cool air as required. It is often a good investment, especially in a small or open-plan kitchen. A cooker hood also reduces cooking smells and steam, but it is fairly expensive and cannot be fitted over a cooker which has an eye-level grill.

Plumbing An adequate supply of hot and cold water and efficient drainage are essential if food is to be prepared and served in hygienic conditions. A double sink is ideal, funds and space permitting, as it allows the washing up to be done in one sink and rinsing in the other. It is also handy for preparing vegetables, especially if a waste disposal unit can be fitted.

Whether it is a double or single sink, a flat surface for stacking dishes is needed on one side and a grooved draining board on the other. A waterproof splash back should be fitted along the back.

Lighting The cooker and sink are best placed so as to get as much daylight as possible. For artificial lighting, separate spotlights for the stove, sink and work surfaces are very efficient when well-placed. Fluorescent strip lighting is cheaper to run and does not cast any shadows, but care must be taken in choosing the tubes as some colours give a blanched appearance to cooked food, which is misleading.

Kitchen Fitments The kitchen fitments should be arranged as far as possible so the food can be moved easily from the larder and refrigerator to the work surface and sink for preparation, then to the cooker and finally to the dining table. The relevant tools should be grouped handy to each work place; saucepans and ovenware next to the cooker, cleaning gear by the sink and so on. The electric blender or mincer should be installed on a work surface or at least readily accessible underneath it, or it will languish little used. Also make sure you have sufficient well placed electric points for your various pieces of equipment.

Try to avoid 'dead' storage space — inaccessible corners in cupboards will get dirty, wall units which are too high can cause accidents. The sink and work surfaces should be at a comfortable height varied according to the job to be done. If there is not enough room for a table and chair, a well-designed kitchen stool incorporating folding steps which will also provide a foot rest, will enable you to sit at ease when peeling or chopping food.

A washable, durable surface on the fitments and walls, and a non-slip, stain-resistant floor covering are essential. Anti-condensation paint on the ceiling is also helpful.

Decorating and furnishing the kitchen is very much a matter of personal taste. The natural wood finishes now fashionable enable one to change colour schemes without restrictions when redecorating or replacing curtains.

Choosing the cooker

The choice of cooker depends first on the type of fuel available — gas, piped or bottled, electricity, solid fuel or oil. Fuel storage cookers like the Aga or Raeburn are often preferred in rural areas as in addition to cooking, they also heat water, warm the kitchen and dry clothes. In town, gas or electricity is the usual choice, or in combination. In a large kitchen you can install a split level cooker with a gas hot plate and electric oven or vice versa and still have adequate working surfaces.

Recent models of gas cookers use electricity for the spark ignition, which is replacing the energy-wasting pilot lights, and also for the optional extras like revolving spits and auto-timers, which switch the oven on and off in your absence. For this, you will need an electric point adjacent to the gas cooker.

The main feature which differentiates the gas from the electric cookers is that a gas oven is hotter at the top than the bottom; so you can bake or roast at the top, casserole in the centre and slow cook on the bottom, cooking three different dishes at the same time. In an electric oven the heat is more evenly distributed. This has been turned to advantage in the fan-assisted model which re-cycles the heat so the temperature is the same on all four shelves which is ideal for batch-cooking.

Manufacturers of both gas and electric cookers have improved the cleanability features. Removable spillage bowls on gas cookers and flat ceramic tops on electric hot plates are recent developments. Easy-cleaning oven linings are a welcome improvement.

Ovenware and saucepans

It is essential to use roasting tins and baking trays which are the right size for the oven. There should be enough room to allow the heat to circulate round the sides of the dishes, or the food will scorch at the edges.

It is important to choose saucepans which have a thick base as thin pans will buckle over high heat on any cooker. Well insulated handles are also important.

Casseroles which are flameproof are more versatile than the ovenproof glass and pottery ones as they can be used to brown meat on the hotplate, simmer in the oven and are pretty enough to put on the table, so saving a lot of washing up. Non-stick linings to both casseroles and saucepans are more expensive but very helpful to the home cook.

Shallow ovenproof gratin dishes for poaching and baking fish, vegetables etc, soufflé and ramekins need not be flameproof, but should be sufficiently attractive to use as part of the table service.

Refrigerators and freezers

It is usually best to choose the largest refrigerator you can accommodate, unless you have a cool, well-ventilated larder. It is not wise to install the refrigerator next to the cooker as it will diminish the efficiency of both appliances.

The Gas and Electricity Boards may not have such a wide selection as the large stores, but their trained staff will be able to give you more detailed information about the functions of the appliances. They can tell you the difference, for instance, between an appliance which has freezer storage but cannot freeze down rapidly raw or cooked food. Never put hot food in a refrigerator or a freezer, as it will raise the internal temperature and cause harmful condensation. It is also well to remember where they will have adequate ventilation. Although cold inside, they produce exterior heat and it is not possible, for instance, to put a freezer into an unventilated cupboard.

Notes

All recipes serve 4 unless otherwise stated
All eggs are grade 3, 4, 5 (standard)
Plain flour and granulated sugar are used unless otherwise stated
All spoon measures are level
Ovens should be preheated to the specified temperature

This open-plan kitchen has most of the requirements for a pleasant and efficient working place: good ventilation and lighting, well-situated sink unit and ample work surfaces.

The Store Cupboard

Storage facilities and the numbers in a family are variable from one house to another and this will determine the quantity and type of food to be kept in storage. The following list gives guidance on the shelf life of different dry goods and suggestions as to basic perishables.

Code

★★★★ keeps well
★★★ keeps up to 6 months
★★ keeps for 2-3 months
★ buy in small quantities
Basic essentials in black type

Beverages

Chocolate ★
Cocoa ★
Coffee, instant and ground
Fruit squash★
Dried skimmed milk★★
Milk, Longlife★
Tea★

Biscuits

Cheese biscuits★
Crispbreads★★
Ratafias★★
Sponge fingers★

Cake & Dessert Decorations★

Chocolate flake
Crystallized angelica
Crystallized ginger
Crystallized orange and
    lemon slices
Crystallized flowers, rose
    petals etc
Glacé cherries
Silver balls

Cans★★★★

Fish — anchovy fillets
    Salmon
    Sardines
    Tuna
Fruit — assorted
Juices — orange
    Grapefruit
    Tomato
Meat — **corned beef**
    Ham
    Liver pâté
    Stewed beef
    Tongue
Milk — **evaporated**
    Condensed

Soups — **consommé**
    Cream of chicken
    Cream of mushroom
    Game
Vegetables — **beans** —
    butter, red kidney, baked
    Carrots, baby
    Chestnut purée,
        unsweetened
    Peas
    Pimentos
    Spinach, leaf and purée
    Tomatoes, peeled
    Tomato paste

Cereals

Barley, pearl ★★★★
Breadcrumbs, dried★★
Cornflakes, etc.★
Ground rice★★★
Lentils and split peas★★★
Oatmeal, medium★★★
Oats, rolled★★
Pasta, macaroni, noodles,
    etc.★★★
Rice, long and short grain★★★
Sago, tapioca★★★
Semolina★★★

COLOURINGS★★★★

Cochineal
Colouring Set

Dried Fruit★★

Apple rings
Apricots
Candied peel — mixed,
    citron
Currants
Dates
Prunes
Raisins, seedless
Sultanas

Dried Vegetables★★★

Beans, butter and haricot
Garlic, flaked
Onion, flaked
Potato, instant

Essences★★★★

Almond or ratafia
Lemon
Orange
Peppermint
Vanilla

Flours★★★

Cornflour
Custard Powder
Plain flour
Self-raising flour
Strong flour
Wholemeal flour
Potato flour
Rice flour

Herbs (Fresh★, Frozen★★, Dried★★★)

Basil
Bayleaf
Chives
Garlic
Marjoram
Mint
Mixed dried
Parsley
Rosemary
Sage
Savory
Tarragon
Thyme

Nuts

Almonds, whole★★, flaked★,
    ground★
Cashew★
Coconut, shredded★★
Hazel★
Peanuts★★
Pistachio★★
Walnuts★

Pickles★★★

Capers
Gherkins
Olives, green, black, stuffed
Onions, silverskin

Preserves

Apricot★★★
Black cherry★★★
Blackcurrant★★★

Cranberry jelly★★★
Golden syrup★★★★
Honey★★★
Lemon curd★★
Marmalade★★★
Mincemeat★★
Raspberry★★★
Redcurrant jelly★★★
Stem ginger★★★
Strawberry★★★
Treacle★★★★

Raising Agents

Baking powder★★
Bicarbonate of soda★★
Cream of tartar★★
Yeast, dried★★★

Sauces

Anchovy★★
Mango chutney★★
Mayonnaise★
Tabasco★★★
Tomato ketchup★★
Tomato chutney★★
Worcestershire sauce★★★

Spices

Allspice★★★
Caraway seeds★★★
Cayenne★★★
Chilli powder★★★★
Cinnamon★★★
**Cloves, whole and
    ground**★★★
Coriander seeds★★★
**Curry powder and
    paste**★★★
Ginger, ground★★★
Mace and **nutmeg**★★★
Mustard, **ground** and
    seeds★★★★
Paprika★★
Pepper, black and white★★
Poppy seeds★★★
Saffron★★★
Salt, fine and coarse★★
Sesame seeds★★★

Sugars

Caster★★★★
Demerara★★
Granulated★★★★
Icing★
Lump★★★★
Soft dark brown★

Sundries

Bouillon cubes, beef,
   chicken★★
Continental mustard★★
Cherries maraschino★★★
Chocolate, plain, dessert★
Gelatine, powdered★★★
Jellies, lemon, raspberry etc.★★★
Meat and yeast extracts★★★★
Oil, olive and corn★★★
Parmesan cheese, grated★
Vinegar, cider, wine,
   tarragon, malt★★★★

Basic Perishables

(Best kept in refrigeration)
Bacon, green or smoked
Cheese, Cheddar etc.
Eggs
Fats — butter
   Vegetable shortening
   Lard
   Margarine
   Shredded suet
Milk and cream
Soured cream
Yoghurt
Lemons
Parsley
Yeast, fresh

Cooking Tools

A set of good, serviceable tools is as essential to the cook as it is to any other craftsman. In addition to the basic necessities, the choice will be determined by the type and extent of the cooking to be undertaken, as well as individual preferences. On the following list, indication is given of those tools which are essential and other tools which are very useful to have and a few optional extras.

Code
- *** Basic essentials
- ** Useful additions
- * Extras

Cutting Tools
- *** Chef's knives (2 sizes)
- *** Carving knife and fork
- *** Bread knife (serrated)
- *** Vegetable knife
- *** Tomato knife (serrated)
- ** Grapefruit knife (curved)
- * Crinkle chip cutter
- *** Swivel peeler
- *** Apple corer and peeler (reversible)
- * Ball scoop (for potatoes and melons)
- ** Cherry/olive stoner
- ** Egg slicer
- *** Kitchen scissors
- *** Knife sharpener (with grinder wheels)
- * Mandolin slicer

Spoons and Forks
- *** Cook's spoon
- *** Cook's fork
- *** Draining spoon
- ** Skimmer
- ** Ladle
- *** Wooden spoons (3 sizes)

Mincers, Graters and Shredders
- * Mouli-parsmint (for herbs)
- * Mouli-grater (for nuts and cheese)
- *** Grater — stainless steel, 4 sides (coarse, medium, fine, very fine)

- ** Zester (for citrus fruit)
- * Garlic press
- *** Salt and pepper mills
- * Pestle and mortar

Sieves and Strainers
- *** Wire sieves (2 sizes)
- ** Conical sieve (chinois, for liquids)
- * Gravy strainer (oval sauceboat shape)
- *** Colander (plastic or metal)
- ** Mouli-légumes (3 blades, for soups and purées)
- *** Tea and coffee strainer
- ** Sugar sifter
- *** Flour sifter
- ** Lemon squeezer

Whisks
- ** Balloon whisk
- *** Rotary whisk

Weighing and Measuring Equipment
- *** Measuring jugs (2 sizes)

- ** Measuring spoon set
- *** Scales
  Thermometers —
  - ** Fat/sugar
  - * Meat
  - ** Fridge/freezer
  - * Oven

Pastry Making Equipment
- *** Pastry board
- *** Rolling pin
- *** Pastry brushes (2 sizes)
- *** Pie dishes (deep)
- *** Pie plates (shallow)
- *** Pie funnel
- *** Flan rings (plain and/or fluted)
- * Tartlet tins
- ** Cooling tray

Baking Equipment
- *** Baking sheets
- ** Bun tins (1 set)
- *** Cake tins with detachable base
- *** Loaf tins (2 sizes)
- *** Sandwich tins (1 pair)
- ** Swiss roll tins

*** Roasting tins (2 sizes)
* Basting syringe

Pots and Pans

*** Saucepans (3 sizes)
** Steamer
*** Kettle
*** Frying pan
** Omelette pan
*** Casseroles with lids (oven and/or flameproof)
** Gratin dishes
* Fish kettle

Moulds

** Jelly moulds (metal)
* Ring mould
*** Soufflé dishes (2 sizes)
** Ramekin dishes (set of 6)
* Dariole moulds

Openers

*** Can opener (solids)
** Can opener (liquids)
* Sardine tin master key
* Screw top jar opener
*** Corkscrew

General Equipment

*** Mixing bowls (2 sizes)
*** Pudding bowls (3 sizes)
*** Chopping board
** Concave spatula
*** Fish slice
** Kichamajig
** Palette knife
** Vegetable brush
** Forcing bag
** Nozzles

*** Skewers
** Funnel
** Nut cracker

Kitchen Stationery

*** Aluminium foil
*** Cling film
*** Greaseproof paper
*** Paper towels
*** Plastic food bags
*** String

Cleaning Utensils

*** Dish mop
*** Absorbent kitchen cloths
** Saucepan mops
*** Scourers
*** Tea cloths

Storage Containers

*** Bread bin
*** Biscuit tin
*** Plastic containers for fridge
*** Storage jars for fat and oil
*** Storage jars for dry foods

1 Kitchen scissors
2 Swivel peeler
3 Fluted flan ring
4 Fat/sugar thermometer
5 Cherry/olive stoner
6 Vegetable knife and chef's knife
7 Knife sharpener
8 Zester
9 Garlic press
10 Skimmer
11 Fish slice
12 Kichamajig
13 Mouli-legumes
14 Four-sided grater

Stocks and Soups Basic Stocks

A full-bodied, well-flavoured stock made with fresh bones, vegetables and herbs is the basis of many good soups and sauces. The bones of roasted joints or poultry may be used, but the flavour will be improved by the addition of meat trimmings or giblets. Use strongly flavoured vegetables, such as turnips and parsnips, with discretion, and omit potatoes which cloud the stock.

All stock should be cooled quickly and kept covered to avoid contamination. Store stock in a cool place, preferably the refrigerator. Boil it up every two days to prevent fermentation. Stock made with onion will ferment more quickly than stock made without onion. For freezing: reduce the stock by boiling (to concentrate the flavour). When the stock is cold, store it in small containers for convenience in sauce making.

White Stock
For light-coloured soups and sauces

METRIC	IMPERIAL
approx. ½ kg veal, lamb or chicken bones	*approx. 1 lb veal, lamb or chicken bones*
approx. 1 ¾ litres cold water	*approx. 3 pints cold water*
1 onion, peeled and sliced	*1 onion, peeled and sliced*
2 carrots, scraped and sliced	*2 carrots, scraped and sliced*
1 stalk celery, washed and chopped	*1 stalk celery, washed and chopped*
bouquet garni	*bouquet garni*
1 teaspoon salt	*1 teaspoon salt*
6-8 peppercorns	*6-8 peppercorns*

YIELD APPROX. 1¼ LITRES/2 PINTS

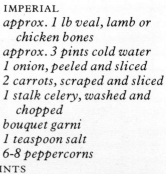

Step 1 Ask the butcher to chop large bones such as knuckle of veal. This will release the gelatine during cooking and give "body" to the stock. Remove any fat from the bones, wash and place them in a large pan. Cover with water and bring to the boil. This is called "blanching".

Step 2 When water boils and scum rises to the surface, remove the scum carefully with a skimmer. Add the prepared vegetables, bouquet garni, salt and peppercorns. Cover and simmer gently for 4-6 hours on top of the stove or in a slow oven.

Step 3 Strain the stock through a large sieve into a cold bowl. Discard the bones and vegetables and allow the stock to cool. If meat bones have been used, leave the stock until it is quite cold as the fat will solidify into a cake on top of the stock and can be easily lifted off.

Step 4 The fat of chicken stock will rise to the surface as it cools, but will not harden. Remove it by drawing sheets of kitchen or tissue paper carefully across the surface of the stock until it is clear. Cover the bowl and chill quickly.

Scots Broth

This country soup is traditionally made with neck of mutton, whatever root vegetables are available and pearl barley. Sometimes the vegetable broth is served first and the meat separately with boiled potatoes, but usually the boned lamb and vegetables are combined to make a hearty meat soup as in this recipe.

METRIC	IMPERIAL
¾ kg neck of lamb, scrag and middle neck	1½ lb neck of lamb, scrag and middle neck
2¼ litres cold water or white stock	4 pints cold water or white stock
salt	salt
freshly ground black pepper	freshly ground black pepper
2 carrots, scraped and diced	2 carrots, scraped and diced
1 turnip, peeled and diced	1 turnip, peeled and diced
1 parsnip or small swede, peeled and diced	1 parsnip or small swede, peeled and diced
1 large onion, peeled and chopped	1 large onion, peeled and chopped
2 leeks, washed and thinly sliced	2 leeks, washed and thinly sliced
3 tablespoons pearl barley	3 tablespoons pearl barley
3 tablespoons chopped parsley, to garnish	3 tablespoons chopped parsley, to garnish

Ask the butcher to chop the neck of lamb into joints. Trim off all fat and put all the meat in a large pan. Cover with the water and add salt and pepper to taste. Bring to the boil and skim. Cover with a lid and simmer gently for 1 hour. Add the prepared vegetables and barley and continue cooking gently for a further hour or until the meat and vegetables are tender.

Lift the lamb from the stock with a slotted spoon, take the meat off the bones and cut into small pieces. Remove the fat from the soup with kitchen paper or lift off when the stock is cold and the fat is solid. Add the meat to the soup and reheat thoroughly. Serve garnished with chopped parsley.

Scots Broth

Brown Stock

For dark-coloured soups and sauces

METRIC	IMPERIAL
½ kg beef or veal bones, chopped	1 lb beef or veal bones, chopped
2 tablespoons dripping or butter	2 tablespoons dripping or butter
approx. 1 ¾ litres water	approx. 3 pints water
1 teaspoon salt	1 teaspoon salt
6-8 peppercorns	6-8 peppercorns
bouquet garni	bouquet garni
1 onion, peeled and sliced	1 onion, peeled and sliced
2 carrots, scraped and sliced	2 carrots, scraped and sliced
1 stalk celery, washed and chopped	1 stalk celery, washed and chopped

YIELD APPROX. 1¼ LITRES/2 PINTS

Trim any fat from the bones. Heat the dripping or butter in a roasting pan in a preheated oven at 200°C, 400°F or gas mark 6 and brown the bones for 30 to 40 minutes. Drain on kitchen paper. Put the bones into a large pan, cover with water and bring to the boil. Skim (see White stock), add salt, peppercorns, bouquet garni and vegetables. Cover and simmer gently for 4 to 6 hours. Strain, cool until the fat is set and remove it. Cover the stock and chill.

French Onion Soup

METRIC	IMPERIAL
½ kg Spanish onions	1 lb Spanish onions
50 g unsalted butter or lard	2 oz unsalted butter or lard
1¼ litres good brown stock	2 pints good brown stock
salt	salt
freshly ground black pepper	freshly ground black pepper
TOPPING	TOPPING
4 slices French bread cut 2 cm thick	4 slices French bread cut ¾ in thick
40 g butter	1½ oz butter
100 g Gruyère or Cheddar Cheese, grated	4 oz Gruyère or Cheddar Cheese, grated

Peel and thinly slice the onions. Heat the butter or lard in a heavy saucepan, add the onions, stir well and cover with a lid. Cook over gentle heat, stirring occasionally, until the onions are softened. Remove the lid and fry the onions until turning golden. Pour in the stock and bring to the simmer. Cover and cook gently for 30 minutes. Add salt and pepper to taste.

Spread the bread slices with butter and cover with grated cheese, reserving some cheese for serving. Bake in a preheated oven at 200°C, 400°F or gas mark 6 until the bread is crisp and the cheese has melted. Alternatively, toast under the grill.

Place a bread slice (croûte) in each soup bowl and pour hot soup over it. Serve immediately and hand the remaining grated cheese in a separate bowl for sprinkling over the soup.

Game Stock

For game soups and sauces

Use the carcass and giblets of game birds, or the bones of hare or venison, and follow the recipe for Brown stock.

Game Soup

METRIC	IMPERIAL
50 g pickled belly of pork or streaky bacon	2 oz pickled belly of pork or streaky bacon
50 g butter or lard	2 oz butter or lard
1 onion, peeled and chopped	1 onion, peeled and chopped
2 stalks celery, washed and chopped	2 stalks celery, washed and chopped
100 g mushrooms, washed and chopped	4 oz mushrooms, washed and chopped
½ teaspoon mixed dried herbs	½ teaspoon mixed dried herbs
50 g flour	2 oz flour
2 tablespoons port or sherry	2 tablespoons port or sherry
750 ml good game stock	1¼ pints good game stock
salt	salt
freshly ground pepper	freshly ground pepper
lemon juice to taste	lemon juice to taste

Game Soup; French Onion Soup

Remove the rind from the pickled pork or bacon rashers and dice the meat. Fry it gently in a heavy pan until the fat runs. Add the butter or lard and fry the onion, celery and mushrooms until they start changing colour. Add the herbs. Remove the pan from the heat and stir in the flour. Return the pan to the heat and fry briskly, stirring continuously, until the vegetables are nicely browned.

Remove the pan from the heat and blend in the port or sherry. Stir in the stock and return the pan to the heat. Bring to the simmer and cook gently for 20 to 30 minutes until the celery is tender. Add salt and pepper and sharpen to taste with lemon juice.

Serve the soup as it is or if a smoother texture is preferred, put it in a blender or through a mouli-légumes (p. 20). Garnish with croûtons of French bread or miniature Herb dumplings (p. 51).

Court Bouillon (Fish Stock)

For soups, sauces and poaching fish

Fish stock is called *court bouillon* (quick bouillon) because it is cooked for a short time only. If the bones are cooked for more than 30 minutes, the stock begins to be gelatinous and sticky. Court bouillon is used for soups and sauces and for poaching fish. The ingredients can be varied according to the fish available. For a sauce, it is best to strain the stock and reduce it by rapid boiling to concentrate the flavour. This is called a fish *fumet*.

METRIC	IMPERIAL
½-¾ kg fish trimmings, bones, skin, head, etc.	1-1½ lb fish trimmings, bones, skin, head etc.
1 medium onion, peeled and sliced	1 medium onion, peeled and sliced
1 carrot, scraped and sliced	1 carrot, scraped and sliced
1 small stalk celery	1 small stalk celery
bouquet garni	bouquet garni
1 teaspoon salt	1 teaspoon salt
10 peppercorns	10 peppercorns
approx. 1¾ litres water	approx. 3 pints water
1 wineglass white wine or	1 wineglass white wine or
1 tablespoon white wine vinegar	1 tablespoon white wine vinegar

YIELD 1.5 LITRES/2½ PINTS

Step 1 Rinse the fish trimmings in cold water and put them in a large pan with the vegetables, bouquet garni, salt and peppercorns. Cover with the cold water and add the wine or vinegar. Bring to the boil and skim off the scum (see White stock, p. 14). Simmer for 20 to 30 minutes.

Step 2 Strain the stock through a large sieve with a fine mesh to catch any small bones. Use the stock for poaching fish or return it to the pan and reduce it by rapid boiling if it is required for a sauce.

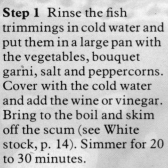

New England Fish Chowder; Fish and Lemon Soup

Fish and Lemon Soup

METRIC	IMPERIAL
1 head halibut, turbot or cod	1 head halibut, turbot or cod
75 g rice	3 oz rice
1¼ litres good Court bouillon	2 pints good Court bouillon
3 egg yolks	3 egg yolks
4 tablespoons lemon juice	4 tablespoons lemon juice
salt	salt
freshly ground pepper	freshly ground pepper
TO GARNISH	TO GARNISH
shredded lettuce or chopped chives	shredded lettuce or chopped chives

Wash the fish head and add it with the rice to the strained hot court bouillon. Bring to the boil, reduce heat and simmer for 20 minutes. Remove the head, flake off the flesh and discard the skin and bones. Crush the flesh with a fork and set it aside. Whisk the egg yolks with the lemon juice in a cup. Mix in 3 to 4 tablespoons of the hot soup and blend the mixture into the soup. Add the flaked fish and reheat, stirring continuously until thickened BUT DO NOT BOIL or the soup will separate. Season with salt and pepper to taste. Serve immediately in soup bowls and garnish with finely shredded lettuce or chopped chives. This is a refreshing soup for summer.

New England Fish Chowder

This is a hearty North American fish soup/stew which is ideal for cold winter days.

METRIC

450 g cod or haddock fillet
600 ml Court bouillon or
    water
salt to taste
50 g pickled belly of pork or
    streaky bacon, diced
50 g butter or bacon fat
225 g potatoes, peeled
1 large onion, peeled and
    chopped
50 g mushrooms, washed and
    sliced
2 tablespoons flour
300 ml milk
lemon juice to taste
freshly ground pepper
2 tablespoons chopped
    parsley

IMPERIAL

1 lb cod or haddock fillet
1 pint Court bouillon or
    water
salt to taste
2 oz pickled belly of pork or
    streaky bacon, diced
2 oz butter or bacon fat
8 oz potatoes, peeled
1 large onion, peeled and
    chopped
2 oz mushrooms, washed and
    sliced
2 tablespoons flour
½ pint milk
lemon juice to taste
freshly ground pepper
2 tablespoons chopped
    parsley

Wash the fish and cut it into 4 pieces. Bring the court bouillon or water to the boil, add the fish and simmer gently for 10 minutes. Lift the fish out and flake it roughly, discarding any skin and bones. Reserve 450 ml/¾ pint of the court bouillon. In a thick pan, fry the pickled pork or bacon gently until the fat runs and the meat crisps, then add the butter or bacon fat.

Cut the potatoes roughly into cubes and add them to the pan with the onion and mushrooms. Fry slowly for 5 minutes. Remove the pan from the heat, blend in the flour and gradually stir in the milk. Return the pan to the heat and cook, stirring continuously until the liquid thickens. Gradually mix in the reserved court bouillon and bring to the simmer. Cook until the potatoes are soft, then add the fish and cook gently for 5 minutes. Sharpen with lemon juice and add salt and freshly ground pepper to taste. Stir in the parsley. Serve with croûtons of French bread.

Thick Soups

These soups are thickened either with a purée of starchy vegetables or, for cream soups, with a butter and flour roux (p. 152).

Purée Soups

Vegetables such as potatoes, peas and beans are cooked in meat or vegetable stock and then put through a mouli-légumes or an electric blender. The purée is thinned to soup consistency with additional stock or milk and is sometimes garnished with a swirl of cream.

Cream Soups

The richer soups are made with less starchy vegetables, such as cauliflower, celery, mushrooms, asparagus or watercress, which are chopped and lightly fried in butter.

The vegetables may be blended with flour to make a roux and then stock and/or milk is added and cooking is continued until the vegetables are tender. This soup can be puréed or not as required.

Alternatively, the fried vegetables are cooked until tender in stock or a mixture of milk and stock, then puréed and enriched with a mixture (liaison) of egg yolk and cream.

Vichyssoise

This French soup can be served hot as a simple family soup (when it is known as Potage à la Bonne Femme) or cold, made into a smooth purée, well chilled and generously laced with cream.

METRIC	IMPERIAL
½ kg leeks	1 lb leeks
½ kg potatoes, peeled and sliced	1 lb potatoes, peeled and sliced
1 medium onion, peeled and sliced	1 medium onion, peeled and sliced
50 g butter or margarine	2 oz butter or margarine
900 ml good chicken stock	1½ pints good chicken stock
salt	salt
freshly ground white pepper	freshly ground white pepper
150 ml single cream	¼ pint single cream
TO GARNISH	TO GARNISH
snipped chives or chopped parsley	snipped chives or chopped parsley

Trim the roots off the leeks and discard the coarse outer leaves. Finely slice the white part and about 5 cm/2 inches of the green and wash thoroughly. Fry the vegetables gently in the butter or margarine in a covered pan until softened. Add the stock and cook for 40 to 45 minutes. Put through the medium grid of a mouli-légume or liquidize in a blender until very smooth. To serve hot, reheat and sprinkle with chopped parsley.

To serve cold, chill thoroughly and adjust the seasoning. Just before serving, swirl in the cream and serve garnished with snipped chives.

Passing vegetables through a mouli-legumes to make a purée soup

Mixed Country Vegetable Soup

METRIC	IMPERIAL
2 rashers streaky bacon	2 rashers streaky bacon
50 g butter or margarine	2 oz butter or margarine
1 large onion, peeled and thinly sliced	1 large onion, peeled and thinly sliced
100 g leeks, white part, washed and chopped	4 oz leeks, white part, washed and chopped
2-3 stalks celery, washed and chopped	2-3 stalks celery, washed and chopped
50 g mushrooms, washed and chopped	2 oz mushrooms, washed and chopped
100 g carrots, scraped and diced	4 oz carrots, scraped and diced
100 g parsnips or swedes, peeled and diced	4 oz parsnips or swedes, peeled and diced
100 g Jerusalem artichokes or turnips, peeled and diced	4 oz Jerusalem artichokes or turnips, peeled and diced
2-3 tablespoons flour	2-3 tablespoons flour
300 ml milk	½ pint milk
250 ml tomato juice	8 fl oz tomato juice
or	or
225 g tomatoes, skinned and chopped	8 oz tomatoes, skinned and chopped
1 tablespoon chopped fresh parsley	1 tablespoon chopped fresh parsley
½ teaspoon mixed dried herbs	½ teaspoon mixed dried herbs
salt	salt
freshly ground black pepper	freshly ground black pepper
approx. 450 ml white stock or water	approx. ¾ pint white stock or water
lemon juice to sharpen	lemon juice to sharpen
croûtons or grated cheese for serving	croûtons or grated cheese for serving

Remove the rind and gristle from the bacon and dice the rashers. Melt the butter or margarine and fry the bacon, onion, leeks, celery and mushrooms until softened but do not allow them to brown. Add the prepared root vegetables and fry gently for 5 minutes.

Remove the pan from the heat and stir in sufficient flour to absorb the fat. Blend in the milk and stir over moderate heat until the liquid has thickened. Add tomato juice or tomatoes, the herbs and salt and pepper to taste. Bring to the simmer and thin as required with water or stock.

Cover and cook over gentle heat for about 45 minutes or until the vegetables are tender. Taste and adjust the seasoning and sharpen to taste with lemon juice. The soup can be served with a bowl of croûtons or grated cheese.

Variation

Cream of Vegetable Soup
Put the soup through a mouli-légumes or blender. Reheat and thin to desired consistency with water or white stock and enrich with 3 to 4 tablespoons single cream.

Serve sprinkled with chopped fresh parsley or chives and fried croûtons.

Vichyssoise; Mixed Country Vegetable Soup

Sauces White Roux Sauces

A roux is melted butter or margarine and flour, usually in equal quantities, blended together to make the basis for a sauce. A liquid, milk and/or stock, is then gradually added. It is very important that the flour is not blended into the fat when the pan is over the heat because the starch grains will burst and cook into lumps. Draw the pan off the heat before mixing in the flour and when blending in the liquid. Return the pan to the heat and stir all the time until the sauce thickens; it should then be beautifully smooth in texture. Should it become lumpy, it may be because you have not stirred carefully over the bottom of the pan. In this case, remove the pan from the heat and whisk until smooth with a rotary or balloon whisk.

White Sauce

Quantities for 300 ml/½ pint

Pouring Sauce
25 g/1 oz butter, 25 g/1 oz flour, 300 ml/½ pint liquid.

Coating Sauce
50 g/2 oz butter, 50 g/2 oz flour, 300 ml/½ pint liquid.

Binding Sauce (Panada)
100 g/4 oz butter, 100 g/4 oz flour, 300 ml/½ pint liquid.

Coating Sauce

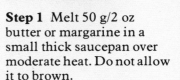 

Step 1 Melt 50 g/2 oz butter or margarine in a small thick saucepan over moderate heat. Do not allow it to brown.

Step 2 Remove the pan from the heat, add 50 g/2 oz flour and stir with a wooden spoon until the butter and flour are smoothly blended.

Step 3 Gradually stir in 300 ml/½ pint milk; keep the pan off the heat or sauce will thicken unevenly and be lumpy. Season to taste with salt and freshly ground pepper or ground nutmeg.

Step 4 Return the pan to the heat and stir steadily until sauce thickens. Simmer gently for 4-5 minutes until the flour is cooked. If there are any lumps, whisk until smooth. Coat the back of the wooden spoon with sauce to check the consistency.

Variations

Anchovy Sauce *(For fish)*
Add 1 to 2 teaspoons anchovy essence to Pouring sauce made with 150 ml/¼ pint milk and 150 ml/¼ pint court bouillon.

Béchamel Sauce *(Use in place of White sauce)*
Heat 1 small peeled onion, 1 bay leaf, 8 peppercorns in 300 ml/½ pint milk for 20 minutes, strain, and use for Pouring sauce.

Alternatively use 150 ml/¼ pint each of milk and well-flavoured White stock (p. 14).

For rich Béchamel, reduce sauce by simmering for 8-10 minutes and finish with 3-4 tablespoons cream.

Caper Sauce *(For lamb and pork)*
Add 1 tablespoon finely chopped capers and 1 teaspoon caper liquid to 300 ml/½ pint Coating sauce.

Cheese Sauce *(For vegetables, fish, chicken, pasta)*
Add 50-75 g/2-3 oz grated cheese to 300 ml/½ pint Coating sauce. Season with 1 teaspoon French mustard and paprika to taste.

Egg Sauce *(For fish and chicken)*
Add 2 chopped, hard-boiled eggs and 1 tablespoon chopped fresh parsley or chives to 300 ml/½ pint Pouring sauce. Season well with salt and freshly ground pepper.

Lemon Sauce *(For vegetables, fish, chicken)*
Add 2 tablespoons lemon juice to 300 ml/½ pint Pouring sauce.

Mustard Sauce *(For fish)*
Add 1-2 tablespoons continental mustard to 300 ml/½ pint Pouring sauce.

Parsley Sauce *(For vegetables, fish and chicken)*
Add 2 tablespoons finely chopped fresh parsley to 300 ml/½ pint Pouring or Coating sauce.

Sour Cream Sauce *(For vegetables, fish, chicken, veal)*
Add 4 tablespoons soured cream to 300 ml/½ pint Coating sauce.

Cheese Sauce poured over cooked leeks, sprinkled with grated cheese and browned under the grill; Egg Sauce coating chicken pieces; Anchovy Sauce with cod steaks

Brown Roux Sauces

These sauces are made by the same method as White sauce but the flour is cooked with the fat until the roux is a rich caramel colour, and brown stock is used instead of milk or white stock.

Thick Gravy (For Roast Joints)

This is the simplest form of brown roux sauce. Carefully pour off the fat from the roasting pan until only 2 tablespoons are left with the juices from the joint. Stir in 1-2 tablespoons flour to absorb the fat and fry, stirring steadily, until well-browned.

Gradually blend in about 300 ml/½ pint brown stock or vegetable liquid and cook briskly for about 5 minutes until the sauce has thickened. Season to taste with salt and pepper.

Variation

Onion Gravy

Peel and chop a large onion. Cook until softened in 2 tablespoons fat, add 2 tablespoons of flour and continue as for Thick gravy.

Variations of Espagnole Sauce, from the left: Burgundy Sauce; Sauce Robert; Bigarade Sauce; Madeira Sauce

Espagnole Sauce

This classic sauce is the basis of many rich brown sauces. It is made by frying a mixture of chopped vegetables and ham (called a *mirepoix*), then thickening with flour which is cooked to a rich caramel colour, before liquid is added.

METRIC	IMPERIAL
1 medium onion	*1 medium onion*
100 g carrots	*4 oz carrots*
50 g mushrooms	*2 oz mushrooms*
1 stalk celery	*1 stalk celery*
2 rashers streaky bacon	*2 rashers streaky bacon*
50 g butter or lard	*2 oz butter or lard*
2-3 tablespoons flour	*2-3 tablespoons flour*
50 ml dry sherry	*2 fl oz dry sherry*
100 ml tomato juice	*4 fl oz tomato juice*
300 ml brown stock	*½ pint brown stock*
pinch of mixed dried herbs	*pinch of mixed dried herbs*
salt	*salt*
freshly ground black pepper	*freshly ground black pepper*
lemon juice to taste	*lemon juice to taste*

Step 1 Peel and chop the onion. Scrape and chop the carrots. Wash and chop the mushrooms and celery. De-rind and chop the bacon. Melt the butter or lard and fry the vegetables and bacon (*mirepoix*) until just golden.

Step 2 Remove the pan from the heat and stir in the flour. Return the pan to the heat and fry, stirring continuously, until the roux is caramel brown. Remove the pan from the heat.

Step 3 Gradually blend in the sherry, tomato juice and then the stock. Use a long-handled spoon to avoid scalding from the steam. Add the herbs, salt, pepper, lemon juice and bring to the simmer, still stirring. Cover and cook gently for 45 minutes or until the vegetables are tender. Stir occasionally to prevent the sauce sticking to the pan.

Step 4 Pass the sauce through a mouli-légumes or sieve. Reheat and taste and adjust the seasoning. If preferred, the sauce can be left unsieved.

Variations (300 ml/½ pint)

Burgundy Sauce *(For steak and game)*

Make brown roux (see Espagnole sauce, Steps 1 and 2) and add 100 ml/4 fl oz red wine instead of sherry before stirring in the tomato juice (Step 3). Continue to follow the Espagnole sauce recipe.

Madeira or Marsala Sauce *(For ham, kidney and liver)*

Follow the recipe for Burgundy sauce using 50 ml/2 fl oz Madeira or Marsala wine instead of red wine. Sweet sherry or Vermouth is an acceptable substitute.

Bigarade Sauce *(For duck, goose, hare and venison)*

Make Burgundy sauce and add the grated rind and juice of 2 oranges and 1 small lemon, 2 tablespoons redcurrant jelly and 50 ml/2 fl oz port. Cook until the jelly is melted and the sauce has slightly reduced.

Sauce Robert *(For pork and lamb)*

Fry 2 tablespoons finely chopped onion in 1 tablespoon melted butter until softened. Add 150 ml/¼ pint dry white wine and 2 teaspoons wine vinegar and boil briskly until reduced by half. Add the mixture to 300 ml/½ pint Espagnole sauce with 1 tablespoon mild French mustard. Add 1 teaspoon sugar or to taste.

Traditional British Sauces

Apple Sauce
For roast pork and sausages

METRIC	IMPERIAL
½ kg apples	1 lb apples
2-3 tablespoons water	2-3 tablespoons water
25 g butter	1 oz butter
sugar to taste	sugar to taste

Peel, core and slice the apples. Put the water in a pan, add the apples, cover and cook gently until soft. Remove the lid, beat until smooth and continue cooking gently until thickened. Stir in the butter and add sugar to taste.

Bread Sauce
For roast chicken, turkey, guinea fowl and pheasant

METRIC	IMPERIAL
1 medium onion	1 medium onion
4 cloves	4 cloves
400 ml milk	¾ pint milk
1 bay leaf	1 bay leaf
salt	salt
freshly ground pepper	freshly ground pepper
75 g diced white bread (without crust)	3 oz diced white bread (without crust)
knob of butter	knob of butter
3-4 tablespoons cream	3-4 tablespoons cream

Peel the onion and stud it with cloves, then put it in a small pan with the milk, bay leaf and salt and pepper. Bring the milk slowly to the boil, remove the pan from the heat, cover and leave in a warm place for 20 minutes to allow the flavours to infuse. Add the bread and, after 20 minutes, remove the onion and bay leaf. Add the butter, whisk until smooth. Stir in the cream, taste and adjust seasoning.

Cumberland Sauce
For baked ham, grilled gammon steak, cold duck, roast venison and hare

METRIC	IMPERIAL
1 orange	1 orange
1 lemon	1 lemon
4 tablespoons redcurrant jelly	4 tablespoons redcurrant jelly
4 tablespoons port	4 tablespoons port
2 teaspoons cornflour	2 teaspoons cornflour
1 tablespoon water	1 tablespoon water

Grate the rind of the orange and lemon very finely with a grater. Squeeze out the juices and put them in a pan with the grated rind and redcurrant jelly. Heat gently and stir until the jelly is dissolved. Add the port. Mix the cornflour with the water and stir in 2 tablespoons of the sauce. Return the mixture to the pan and cook, stirring, until the sauce thickens and becomes clear.

Gooseberry Sauce
For grilled mackerel and pork chops

METRIC	IMPERIAL
225 g gooseberries	8 oz gooseberries
3-4 tablespoons water	3-4 tablespoons water
25 g butter	1 oz butter
sugar to taste	sugar to taste

Top and tail the gooseberries. Put them in a pan with the water, cover and cook until soft. Whisk the gooseberries until smooth and continue cooking until they form a thick purée. Stir in the butter and add sugar to taste.

Horseradish Cream
For roast beef, smoked mackerel and eel

METRIC	IMPERIAL
2 tablespoons grated horseradish	2 tablespoons grated horseradish
150 ml soured cream	¼ pint soured cream
1 teaspoon French mustard	1 teaspoon French mustard
1 teaspoon caster sugar	1 teaspoon caster sugar
salt	salt
freshly ground pepper	freshly ground pepper

Mix the horseradish into the soured cream. Add the mustard and sugar and salt and pepper to taste. Double cream sharpened with 2 teaspoons lemon juice may be used instead of the soured cream.

Mint Sauce
For roast lamb and grilled lamb chops

METRIC/IMPERIAL
1 teacup fresh mint leaves
1 tablespoon caster sugar
2 tablespoons boiling water
approx. 2 tablespoons cider
   vinegar

Chop the mint leaves finely with the caster sugar and put them in a sauceboat. Add the boiling water and stir until the sugar is dissolved. Add sufficient vinegar to cover the mint. Leave to infuse.

Cumberland Sauce; Bread Sauce; Gooseberry Sauce; Horseradish Cream, Mint Sauce; Apple Sauce

Egg-Based Sauces

Egg-based sauces are made with oil if cold and with butter if hot. All require care in making or they will curdle and separate. They can sometimes be retrieved by adding the curdled sauce, a teaspoonful at a time, to a freshly beaten egg yolk.

Mayonnaise

METRIC
2 egg yolks
¼ teaspoon each salt and
    sugar
freshly ground pepper to
    taste
½ teaspoon French mustard
150 ml olive oil
1 tablespoon tarragon
    vinegar
Makes 150 ml/¼ pint

IMPERIAL
2 egg yolks
¼ teaspoon each salt and
    sugar
freshly ground pepper to
    taste
½ teaspoon French mustard
¼ pint olive oil
1 tablespoon tarragon
    vinegar

Tartare Sauce

METRIC
2 teaspoons finely chopped
    capers
2 teaspoons finely chopped
    gherkins
1 teaspoon finely chopped
    shallots
2 tablespoons finely chopped
    fresh parsley
150 ml Mayonnaise
mustard and lemon juice to
    taste

IMPERIAL
2 teaspoons finely chopped
    capers
2 teaspoons finely chopped
    gherkins
1 teaspoon finely chopped
    shallots
2 tablespoons finely chopped
    fresh parsley
¼ pint Mayonnaise
mustard and lemon juice to
    taste

Mix the finely chopped ingredients into the mayonnaise and season to taste with mustard and lemon juice.

Step 1 Stand a small bowl on a teatowel and wrap the towel around the bowl to prevent it sliding about while you are stirring.

Step 2 Put the egg yolks in the bowl with the salt, sugar, pepper and mustard and mix well with a small wooden spoon.

Step 3 Put the oil in a jug and add it to the egg yolks trickle by trickle, while stirring steadily, always in the same direction, to avoid curdling.

Step 4 When the mixture thickens, stir in a little of the vinegar; add the rest when all the oil is used. Taste and adjust the seasoning.

Note: To reduce the cost, up to 50 per cent corn oil can be mixed with the olive oil. Wine or cider vinegar can be used but not malt vinegar. For Lemon mayonnaise, use fresh lemon juice instead of vinegar.

Hollandaise Sauce

Serve warm with fish, chicken, asparagus, artichokes and broccoli.

METRIC	IMPERIAL
2 egg yolks	2 egg yolks
lemon juice to taste	lemon juice to taste
100 g unsalted butter	4 oz unsalted butter
salt to taste	salt to taste
cold water	cold water

Tartare Sauce; Mayonnaise; Mousseline Sauce; Hollandaise Sauce

Step 1 Cut the butter up into small even-sized pieces. Put the egg yolks and 1 tablespoon lemon juice in a bowl over a saucepan of simmering water. Take care the water does not touch the bottom of the bowl. Put a cup of cold water and a teaspoon on the side.

Step 2 Stir the egg yolk and lemon juice together over low heat until the mixture begins to thicken. Stir in the butter, one piece at a time. Allow each piece to melt before adding the next.

Step 3 At the first sign of "scrambling" remove the bowl from the saucepan and add a teaspoon of cold water. Continue adding butter and replace the bowl over saucepan, adding cold water as required. When all the butter is incorporated, remove sauce from the heat and season to taste with salt and lemon juice. Serve at once as it separates when cold.

Mousseline Sauce

Serve warm or cold with fish, chicken and delicate vegetables such as asparagus.

Add 50-75 ml/2-3 fl oz single cream to the finished Hollandaise sauce and extra salt and lemon juice to taste. This sauce can be refrigerated and served cold, or gently reheated over hot water and served warm.

Sweet Dessert Sauces

These sauces, which are served with hot puddings and cold desserts, usually have either an egg custard base or are thickened with cornflour.

Custard

METRIC	IMPERIAL
3 egg yolks	3 egg yolks
1 tablespoon caster sugar	1 tablespoon caster sugar
300 ml milk	½ pint milk
¼ teaspoon vanilla essence	¼ teaspoon vanilla essence

Step 1 Whisk the egg yolks and sugar together in a bowl until they are well blended. In a small saucepan heat the milk until it is nearly boiling.

Step 2 Whisk the heated milk gradually into the egg yolk mixture. Place the bowl over a saucepan of simmering water or pour the mixture into the top of a double saucepan with hot water in the lower container.

Step 3 Stir over the heat until the custard thickens and coats the back of the wooden spoon in a creamy film. If the custard is cooked over direct heat it is very liable to curdle.

Step 4 Add the vanilla essence and more sugar if desired. Strain and serve warm or pour into a cold bowl and allow to cool, stirring occasionally to prevent a skin forming.

Chocolate Sauce served hot over a poached pear; Brandy Butter on a baked apple; Fruit Sauce with ice-cream

Variations

Coffee Custard

Mix 2 teaspoons instant coffee with the sugar and egg yolks before adding the hot milk.

Sherry Custard

Reduce the quantity of milk by 3 tablespoons and add 3 tablespoons sweet sherry to the custard when cooked.

Orange Custard

Finely grate the rind of 1 large orange. Reduce the quantity of milk by 3 tablespoons and infuse the rind in the milk as it heats. Add the strained orange juice to the custard when cooked.

Chocolate Sauce

METRIC	IMPERIAL
1 tablespoon cornflour	1 tablespoon cornflour
1 tablespoon cocoa	1 tablespoon cocoa
2-3 teaspoons caster sugar	2-3 teaspoons caster sugar
300 ml milk	½ pint milk
15 g butter	½ oz butter
¼ teaspoon vanilla essence	¼ teaspoon vanilla essence
sugar to taste	sugar to taste

Blend the cornflour, cocoa and sugar to a thin cream with 4 tablespoons of the measured milk. Heat the remaining milk with the butter until boiling and add it gradually to the cocoa mixture, stirring steadily. Return the mixture to the pan and simmer for 3 minutes, stirring continuously to prevent lumps forming. Flavour with vanilla and add sugar to taste.

Hard Sauces

These are made with butter and sugar, flavoured with brandy, rum or whisky, then chilled and served with hot puddings and tarts.

Brandy Butter

METRIC
100 g unsalted butter
100 g caster sugar
3 tablespoons brandy

IMPERIAL
4 oz unsalted butter
4 oz caster sugar
3 tablespoons brandy

Cream the butter until soft. Beat in the sugar a tablespoon at a time, with a teaspoon of brandy, adding it very gradually so the sauce will not curdle. Chill until hard and serve with Christmas pudding, mince pies, etc.

Cumberland Rum Butter

METRIC
100 g unsalted butter
2 teaspoons grated lemon rind
100 g soft brown sugar
3 tablespoons rum

IMPERIAL
4 oz unsalted butter
2 teaspoons grated lemon rind
4 oz soft brown sugar
3 tablespoons rum

Cream the butter with the lemon rind and beat in the sugar and rum as for Brandy butter. Chill until hard and serve with baked apples, steamed puddings, etc.

Fruit Sauce

Use canned or stewed apricots, plums, raspberries, loganberries, gooseberries or red or black currants for fruit sauces, which are served with hot puddings or chilled and served with cold desserts and ice cream.

METRIC
1 × 425 g can fruit
2 teaspoons cornflour
3 tablespoons reserved fruit juice
sugar and lemon juice to taste

IMPERIAL
1 × 15 oz can fruit
2 teaspoons cornflour
3 tablespoons reserved fruit juice
sugar and lemon juice to taste

Strain the juice from the fruit. Sieve the fruit, measure it and make it up to 300 ml/½ pint with fruit juice and bring to the boil. Blend the cornflour to a smooth paste with the reserved fruit juice and stir it into the sauce. Cook gently, stirring steadily until the sauce thickens and becomes clear. Flavour to taste with sugar and lemon juice. A tablespoon of a fruit liqueur may also be added.

Eggs Basic Methods

Eggs are graded by weight under Common Market regulations into 7 sizes and are priced accordingly. Most recipes are designed for standard eggs (50-60 g), which are European grades 3, 4, 5. In this book, standard eggs are used unless otherwise specified. Eggs are date-stamped by the packing stations with the relevant week number, the week of January 1st being Week 1, so their freshness can be checked when buying. You can test an egg by putting it in a bowl of cold water – if very fresh it will sink to the bottom. If not so fresh, the air pocket at the top of the egg enlarges and the egg will tilt upwards. When broken onto a plate or into a frying pan, a fresh white clings to the yolk, but when stale, the white is thin and spreads quickly away from the yolk. Fresh eggs can be stored for 3 weeks in a cool larder or refrigerator. Whole eggs in the shell cannot be frozen. Separated yolks and whites can be refrigerated or frozen if lightly beaten and closely covered.

Boiling Eggs

Eggs should be at room temperature. If they are very cold, warm them under the hot tap, or prick the rounded end of the shell with a needle to prevent cracking. A teaspoon of salt added to the water will 'set' any escaping white. The water should only simmer, never boil quickly.

Place the eggs in a pan of cold water, bring to boil, turn down to simmer and count the cooking time from then.

SIZE	SOFT	MEDIUM	HARD
Large	3 mins	4 mins	10 mins
Standard	2½ mins	3½ mins	9 mins

Lift the cooked eggs out of the water, tap the shell at one end to allow steam to escape and prevent further cooking. Put hard-boiled eggs in cold water to prevent a grey line forming round the yolk.

Eggs Mornay

Hard-boiled eggs make a nice supper dish served hot. Coat the eggs with Cheese sauce (p. 23), top with bread crumbs and grated cheese and brown under the grill.

Eggs Mayonnaise

Cold hard-boiled eggs coated with Mayonnaise (p. 28) and garnished with lettuce or watercress make an attractive first course.

Coddled Eggs

Put the eggs into boiling water, cover the pan, remove from the heat and leave the egg in the pan for 8 to 10 minutes. The white will be just set and be more digestible for babies and invalids.

Poaching Eggs

An egg for poaching should be broken carefully into a cup or saucer. Heat 2.5 cm/1 inch of water in a shallow pan (a frying pan is suitable). Do not add salt or vinegar or the whites will toughen. Bring the water to a gentle simmer, with the water barely moving, and slide in the egg gently. Cook for about 3 minutes or remove the pan from heat, cover and leave for 3½ to 4 minutes. Lift out with a perforated spoon – when poaching more than one, take eggs out in the order in which they were put in. Drain over a cloth before serving on hot toast spread with butter or anchovy paste or on smoked ham, smoked haddock or spinach purée.

Frying Eggs

Heat a little butter, bacon fat or oil in a frying pan and slide in the egg just before the fat starts to sizzle. Fry gently or the white will be tough. Baste with the hot fat until the white is set but the yolk still soft, about 3 minutes. Lift out carefully with a fish slice and serve with fried or grilled bacon, sausages, hamburgers or corned beef hash.

Scrambling Eggs

Allow 2 eggs per person. Season the eggs to taste with salt and pepper and beat with a fork, not a whisk. Melt a knob of butter in the top of a double boiler or thick, non-stick saucepan and add the eggs. Stir with a wooden spoon over very gentle heat until thick and creamy. Remove from the heat and stir in 1 tablespoon of cream or top of the milk; this will stop the eggs from over-cooking. Serve immediately on buttered toast or fried bread and garnish with a sprig of parsley; for a first course serve on asparagus tips.

Variations

Mix grated cheese, cooked ham or bacon, flaked cooked or smoked fish, crab-meat or prawns into the beaten eggs before cooking. Serve hot or cold in sandwiches, bread rolls or pastry cases.

Baked Eggs

Baked on a plate (Sur le plat)

Preheat the oven to 220°C, 425°F or gas mark 7. Butter and warm individual ovenproof plates in the oven for a minute or two. Break 2 eggs into each plate. Top with 1 tablespoon melted butter or cream, season to taste with salt and pepper and bake for 4 to 5 minutes until the whites are set and the yolks still soft. Serve at once in the dishes.

Variations

Put a slice of cooked ham, sliced smoked sausages or fried sliced mushrooms on the plate and break the eggs on top. When cooked, garnish with fresh parsley sprigs.

Baked Eggs; Scrambled Eggs; Poached Eggs; Fried Egg.
Below left: In a Ramekin (en cocotte)

In Ramekins *(En Cocotte)*

Preheat the oven to 180°C, 350°F or gas mark 4. Butter individual ovenproof ramekin dishes. Put 1 tablespoon cream or top of the milk in each ramekin. Drop in 1 or 2 eggs, season with salt and pepper and put another spoonful of cream or butter on top. Place in a shallow pan with hot water and bake for 8 to 10 minutes until yolks are just set and whites filmy.

Variations

Mix the cream with tomato sauce or ketchup to taste or grated cheese. Alternatively, in the bottom of each ramekin place a layer of minced mushrooms, cooked ham or chicken or buttered shrimps – this is a delicious first course.

Omelettes

French Savoury Omelettes

Allow 2 eggs per person and choose an omelette pan the right size, 18 cm/7 inches for 2 eggs.

An omelette pan has specially rounded sides but a thick frying pan can also be used.

Omelette Fines Herbes

METRIC/IMPERIAL
2 eggs
1 tablespoon chopped fresh
  herbs (parsley, chervil and
  chives)
1 teaspoon water
salt
freshly ground white pepper
small knob of butter

Variations

Cheese Omelette

Mix 2 tablespoons grated cheese into the beaten eggs instead of the chopped herbs.

Stuffed Savoury Omelettes

Sliced mushrooms, chopped ham or bacon, crisp bread croûtons, potato cubes, asparagus tips, spinach purée are all good fillings. Fry the filling in butter and keep warm while you make the omelette. Spoon the filling on top of the omelette just before folding it over. Allow 2-3 tablespoons cooked filling for each person.

Step 1 Beat the eggs with a fork. Mix in the herbs, water and salt and pepper to taste. Heat butter until it sizzles but do not allow it to brown. Pour in beaten eggs.

Step 2 With a fork or a palette knife, draw the mixture from sides to middle of pan and tilt pan so the uncooked egg runs underneath and sets.

Step 3 When the underneath is set but the top still slightly runny, fold the omelette in half (if using 4 eggs, fold the omelette in three).

Turn a 2-egg omelette upside down onto a warm plate. If making a 4-egg omelette, fold it in three and slide it onto a warm plate. Serve immediately.

Step 1 Light the grill or preheat the oven to 220°C, 425°F or gas mark 7. Whisk the egg whites until soft peaks are formed. Whisk the egg yolks with the water and fold into the whites.

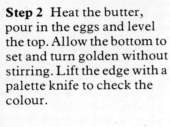

Step 2 Heat the butter, pour in the eggs and level the top. Allow the bottom to set and turn golden without stirring. Lift the edge with a palette knife to check the colour.

Step 3 Put the pan under the grill or in the top of the oven for 1-2 minutes until well risen and setting. Spoon the hot jam down the centre.

Fold the omelette in half over the filling and slide it onto a warm plate. Dust with caster sugar and serve immediately.

Sweet Soufflé Omelette

METRIC	IMPERIAL
2 eggs, separated	*2 eggs, separated*
2 teaspoons water	*2 teaspoons water*
15 g butter	*½ oz butter*
2 tablespoons whole fruit jam, heated	*2 tablespoons whole fruit jam, heated*
caster sugar	*caster sugar*

Variations
Use fresh or canned fruit instead of jam, well sugared or flavoured with liqueur. Alternatively, the finished omelette can be flamed in rum. Use 1 tablespoon rum, warm it, set light to it with a match and pour flaming over the omelette. Serve at once.

Hot Soufflés

The basis of a hot soufflé is a thick roux-based sauce (panada, p. 22) mixed with a sweet or savoury ingredient. Beaten egg yolks and whisked egg whites are then incorporated into the mixture to give it its characteristic light and airy texture when cooked.

Cheese Soufflé

METRIC	IMPERIAL
4 eggs, separated	*4 eggs, separated*
50 g butter or margarine	*2 oz butter or margarine*
50 g flour	*2 oz flour*
150 ml milk	*¼ pint milk*
75 g Cheddar cheese, grated	*3 oz Cheddar cheese, grated*
1 tablespoon grated	*1 tablespoon grated*
* Parmesan cheese*	* Parmesan cheese*
salt	*salt*
freshly ground black pepper	*freshly ground black pepper*
paprika pepper	*paprika pepper*
1 teaspoon French mustard	*1 teaspoon French mustard*

Variations
Mix into the binding sauce before adding the egg yolks:
1. 1 tablespoon chopped parsley, 225 g/8 oz finely minced cooked chicken, turkey or ham, lemon juice and Worcestershire sauce to taste.
2. 225 g/8 oz finely flaked cooked (or canned) salmon, smoked haddock or mackerel, white fish, crab or lobster meat; flavour to taste with finely chopped chervil or parsley, lemon juice and anchovy essence.
3. 225 g/8 oz finely chopped cooked mushroom or spinach or potato purée and flavour to taste with fresh herbs and garlic or onion.

Step 1 Grease an 18 cm/7 inch soufflé dish. Cut a strip of greaseproof paper long enough to wrap around the dish and overlap by 5 cm/2 inches and deep enough to extend 7.5 cm/3 inches above the rim. Secure with string. Preheat oven to 190°C, 375°F or gas mark 5.

Step 2 Make a binding sauce with the butter or margarine, flour and milk (see p. 22). Remove the pan from the heat and stir in the grated cheeses, salt, pepper and paprika pepper to taste, and the mustard. Gradually beat in the egg yolks. In a wide bowl whisk the egg whites until stiff but not brittle. Pour over the cheese sauce, about a third at a time, and fold it in quickly and lightly with a concave spatula or large cook's spoon.

Step 3 Pour the mixture into the prepared soufflé dish: to make the soufflé rise evenly with a "crown" in the centre scoop out a shallow ring round the top about 2.5 cm/1 inch from the rim of the dish.

Step 4 Stand the soufflé dish on a baking tray and place it in the centre of the oven. Bake for about 30 minutes until well risen and golden brown. It should still be slightly soft in the centre. Serve immediately: remove paper at last moment or the soufflé may fall.

Right: Chocolate Soufflé

Chocolate Soufflé

METRIC	IMPERIAL
100 g plain chocolate	4 oz plain chocolate
4 tablespoons black coffee	4 tablespoons black coffee
40 g butter	1½ oz butter
40 g plain flour	1½ oz plain flour
225 ml milk	8 fl. oz milk
50 g caster sugar	2 oz caster sugar
¼ teaspoon vanilla essence	¼ teaspoon vanilla essence
4 egg whites	4 egg whites
3 egg yolks	3 egg yolks
2-3 tablespoons rum or Tia Maria (optional)	2-3 tablespoons rum or Tia Maria (optional)
3 tablespoons icing sugar	3 tablespoons icing sugar

Prepare a 15 cm/6 inch soufflé dish (see step 1, Cheese soufflé) and heat the oven to 190°C, 375°F or gas mark 5. Break up the chocolate into a bowl, add the coffee and place the bowl over a saucepan of boiling water to melt the chocolate. Melt the butter in a small saucepan, remove it from the heat, stir in flour and gradually add the milk. Cook over a gentle heat for three minutes, stirring. Stir the melted chocolate and blend it into the sauce. Stir in the sugar and vanilla essence. Remove the pan from the heat, whisk the egg whites in a large bowl until stiff but still moist. Whisk the egg yolks in a separate bowl and add them gradually to the chocolate sauce. Pour the sauce over the whisked egg whites, about a third at a time, and fold it in quickly and lightly. Fold in the rum or Tia Maria, if used. Pour the mixture into the prepared soufflé dish and scoop out a crown (see Cheese soufflé).

Bake in the centre of the oven for 25-30 minutes until well risen. The soufflé should be crisp on top and slightly soft in the centre. Dredge with sifted icing sugar, remove the paper and serve immediately. If liked, serve with a hot Custard (p. 30) flavoured with vanilla, coffee, sherry or liqueur.

Variation

Hot Fruit Soufflé
Follow the previous recipe but use 300 ml/½ pint fruit purée (apricots, plums, raspberry or loganberry) instead of milk and omit the chocolate. Serve with Fruit sauce (p. 31).

Grilling Meat

Prime cuts of meat only are suitable for grilling, which is so rapid the meat must be tender, and if it is beef, well hung. Even the best quality rump steak, if freshly killed, will be tough, so you need a reliable butcher.

To prepare meat for grilling, remove any skin and surplus fat. Brush with oil or melted butter and season with freshly ground pepper, but no salt as this draws the juice out of the meat. Steak can be beaten with a rolling pin to break down the fibres and tenderize it.

Preheat the grill to the highest heat and put the prepared meat on the greased grid. Cook until the meat is brown on one side, then turn it and brown the other side. This seals in the juices and is sufficient cooking for lamb cutlets and underdone steak. For chops — especially pork and veal — and well done steak, continue cooking at reduced heat until cooked through. Use tongs for turning and do not pierce the meat with a fork. Serve immediately, garnished if liked. Do not attempt to cook grilled meat in advance and keep it warm, as it will dry out and toughen.

The numbers following the meats listed below, identify the meats in the photograph (see key, opposite).

Suitable cuts of meat for grilling are *Beef:* Fillet steak (19) or tournedos (18), rump steak (22), sirloin steak (23), entrecôte (20), T-bone (untrimmed) (21) or porterhouse steak. *Lamb:* Chump chops (10), loin chops (9), neck cutlets (11), steaks cut from fillet end of leg (13), liver (8) and kidney (6 and 7). *Pork:* Fillet (3), spare rib chops (4), loin chops (5), liver (2) and kidney (1). *Veal:* Fillet and leg escalopes (14 and 15), large neck cutlets (17), loin chops (16), liver (12).

Sausages and beefburgers.

Grilling Times

For portions, except bacon rashers, cut approximately 2.5 cm/1 inch thick and weighing 100-200 g/4-8 oz.

MEAT	CUT	COOKING TIME
Beef	Fillet steak and tournedos	7 — 12 minutes
	Rump steak	8 — 14 minutes
	Sirloin and entrecôte	10 — 15 minutes
Lamb	Neck cutlet	8 — 10 minutes
	Chump and Loin chop	8 — 12 minutes
	Leg fillet steak	10 — 15 minutes
	Liver (sliced), kidney	5 — 8 minutes
Pork	Fillet steak	8 — 12 minutes
	Neck cutlets	12 — 15 minutes
	Loin chops	16 — 20 minutes
Veal	Fillet and leg escalopes	8 — 12 minutes
	Neck cutlet	12 — 15 minutes
	Loin chop	16 — 20 minutes
	Liver (sliced)	5 — 8 minutes
Bacon	Rashers (thin)	5 — 8 minutes
Gammon	Steak (1 cm/½ inch)	8 — 10 minutes

Mixed Grill

Serves 2

2 lamb cutlets or loin chops
2 pork sausages
oil for brushing
2 lambs' kidneys
2 large tomatoes
salt

freshly ground black pepper
sugar
butter
4 large mushrooms
2 rashers streaky bacon
watercress for garnish

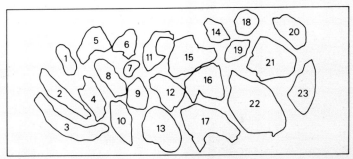

Numbers in this key correspond to the meats listed opposite

Step 1 Trim the cutlets or chops, removing any skin and surplus fat. Place on an oiled grid with the sausages. Brush the cutlets and sausages with oil. Put under a preheated grill and cook until brown (about 5 minutes), turning the sausages as necessary, but not the cutlets.

Step 2 Meanwhile, slit the kidneys down the back, peel off the skin and remove the fatty core with scissors. Skewer them open so they will not curl when cooking. Brush with oil. Halve the tomatoes crossways, not downwards. Season with salt, pepper and sugar to taste and dot with butter. Remove the mushroom stalks, season the black side with salt and pepper and dot with butter.

Step 3 Stretch the bacon rashers with the back of a knife and remove the rind and gristle. Roll up the rashers and skewer them. When the cutlets are brown on the first side, turn with tongs and add the kidneys, bacon rolls, tomatoes and mushrooms. Turn the kidneys, sausages and bacon rolls as necessary but not the cutlets or vegetables.

Step 4 When the cutlets are brown on the second side, place them on a dish or two individual plates and arrange the rest of the mixed grill round them. Top the cutlets with the mint butter, garnish with fresh watercress and serve with Chips (p. 67) or Sauté potatoes (p. 70).

Mint Butter
2 tablespoons fresh mint
50 g/2 oz softened butter
lemon juice to sharpen

Beat the mint into the butter and sharpen to taste with lemon juice. Shape into a roll and chill between sheets of plastic. When hard, cut into slices and use for garnish.

Grilling Fish

Grilling is an excellent way to cook small whole fish weighing 225-275 g/8-10 oz and fillets, cutlets and steaks of larger fish. They may be garnished with Parsley butter (p. 153), lemon wedges and parsley sprigs, and served with grilled tomatoes and/or mushrooms.

Suitable fish for grilling are: *small round fish:* bass, bream (white); herring, mackerel, mullet, trout (oily). *Large round fish* (fillets, cutlets, steaks): cod, haddock, hake, halibut, turbot and salmon (oily). *Flat white fish:* brill, dab, flounder, plaice, sole. *Smoked fish:* kipper, cod and haddock fillet, tuna and finnan haddock.

Make 2 or 3 diagonal cuts on each side of the fish to allow the heat to penetrate quickly and to prevent the skin bursting. Brush white fish with oil or melted butter. This is not necessary for oily fish as the skin will crisp naturally.

Grill fish under a medium heat for 5 minutes or until golden. Turn carefully, brush with oil or butter and cook the other side until the flesh shrinks from the bone at the head end. If liked, serve white fish with Tartare sauce (p. 28); herring and mackerel with Gooseberry sauce (p. 27) and smoked fish with Horseradish cream (p. 27).

Small Round Fish

Remove the scales by scraping with a small knife or scaler from tail to head, under cold running water. Gut the fish (p. 60) and wash the cavity thoroughly under cold running water. Cut off fins with scissors. If leaving the head on, remove the eyes. Dry on kitchen paper.

Fillets, Cutlets and Steaks of Large Round Fish

Skin fillets if wished by laying on a board, skin downwards. Lift the tail, insert a thin sharp knife between the skin and the flesh and, holding the tail skin firmly, gradually saw the flesh off the skin working towards the head. Salt or a net

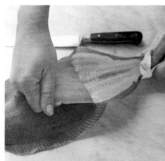

Skinning fillets of large round fish

Scaling round fish

Skinning flat fish

cloth will help to prevent the skin from slipping through your fingers.

Brush fish with oil or melted butter, plain or herb flavoured (p. 153).

Grill for 5-10 minutes, according to thickness. Thin fillets will not require turning and are cooked when the flesh flakes easily. Turn thick pieces, brush with oil and cook the other side. Steaks are ready when the flesh shrinks from the backbone. Season with salt, freshly ground pepper and lemon juice before serving. Garnish with parsley or chervil butter. Serve with Hollandaise or Mousseline sauce (p. 29) if liked.

Small Flat White Fish

Cut off the head, remove the entrails and wash the fish thoroughly. To skin, turn the fish, dark side uppermost, with the tail towards you. Make a slit in the skin just above the tail and raise the skin with a knife. With the right thumb, loosen the skin up the right side. With the left thumb repeat on the left side. Using a cloth, hold the tail firmly and pull the skin off towards the head. The white skin may be left on. Trim off the fins; it is not necessary to score the fish. Brush with butter and grill as for round fish.

Grilled Mackerel

METRIC/IMPERIAL
*4 fresh mackerel weighing
    about 275 g/10 oz each*
8 large mushrooms
salt
freshly ground pepper

1 tablespoon butter
TO GARNISH
lemon and parsley sprigs

Scale the mackerel as described opposite under Small round fish. Clean the mackerel, cutting off the fins, and vandyke the tail (i.e. cut a 'V' in the middle). Remove the eyes from the head.

Cut 3 diagonal slits on each side of the fish. Place on a greased grid and grill under moderate heat for 7 minutes, then turn carefully. Put seasoned mushroom caps, black side uppermost, on grid and dot with butter. Cook the fish until the flesh shrinks from the bone at the head end.

Place the fish and mushrooms on a warm serving dish. Garnish the fish with lemon wedges and mushroom caps, black side uppermost, and small parsley sprigs. Serve with Gooseberry sauce (p. 27) if liked.

1 Plaice	7 Mackerel	13 Kipper
2 Dover sole	8 Finnan haddock	14 Salmon steak
3 Hake	9 Cod fillet	15 Haddock fillet
4 Bream	10 Halibut steak	16 Trout
5 Flounder	11 Grey mullet	17 Smoked cod
6 Turbot steak	12 Smoked haddock fillet	

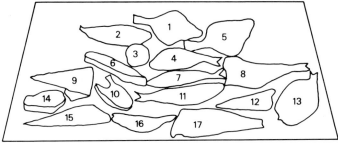

Roasting Oven Roasting: Meat

This popular way of cooking joints of meat is suitable only for prime and tender cuts, such as *Beef:* Sirloin, Wing rib, Fore rib. *Veal:* Leg, Loin, Shoulder, Breast. *Lamb:* Leg, Shoulder, Loin, Best end of neck, Breast. *Pork:* Leg, Loin, Blade, Hand, Belly.

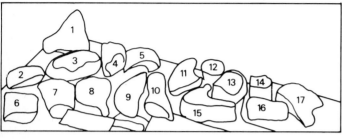

1 Shoulder of pork (hand)
2 Blade of pork
3 Pork fillet (end of leg)
4 Leg of lamb
5 Best end of neck of lamb
6 Belly of pork
7 Loin of pork
8 Shoulder of lamb
9 Breast of lamb
10 Loin of lamb
11 Fore rib of beef
12 Rolled sirloin of beef
13 Beef sirloin on the bone
14 Loin of veal
15 Beef: wing rib
16 Shoulder of veal
17 Breast of veal

Cooking Chart

MEAT	OVEN TEMPERATURE	TIME
Beef (under-done)	220°C, 425°F or gas mark 7	15 mins per ½ kg/1 lb plus 15 mins extra
Beef (well-done)	200°C, 400°F or gas mark 6	20 mins per ½ kg/1 lb plus 20 mins extra
Veal	190°C, 375°F or gas mark 5	25 mins per ½ kg/1 lb plus 25 mins extra
Lamb	200°C, 400°F or gas mark 6	20 mins per ½ kg/1 lb plus 20 mins extra
Pork	220°C, 425°F or gas mark 7	For first 30 mins
	190°C, 375°F or gas mark 5	25 mins per ½ kg/1 lb for remaining time

Boned Joints

Joints which have been boned and rolled require an extra 5 minutes per ½ kg/1 lb. Stuffed joints should be weighed after boning and stuffing and timed as boned joints. Use the bones from the joint to make Stock (p. 14) for gravy.

Method

Weigh the meat and work out the cooking time. Heat the oven to the required temperature. A preheated oven is necessary to brown the joint quickly and seal in the juices. Place the joint in a roasting tin greased with the relevant dripping; beef, lamb or pork. Store dripping from different meats separately, not mixed. Arrange the joint so that the thickest layer of fat is on the top and spread with a little dripping.

Cook the meat in the centre of the oven and time it according to the chart. Baste lean joints from time to time with the fat in the roasting pan to improve the flavour and texture. Test to see whether meat is done by inserting a skewer in the flesh, not in the fat, and press out some juice. If the juice is red the meat is underdone, which may be suitable for beef. When the meat is cooked through, the juice will be amber-coloured.

A meat thermometer can be used to show when meat is rare, medium or well done. Insert the thermometer in the thickest part of the joint (it must NOT touch the bone) before the joint is put in the oven. Place the cooked joint on a warm serving dish. The meat will be easier to carve if it is allowed to cool slightly and set. To make thick gravy see p. 24; for thin gravy see recipe for Roast stuffed blade of pork.

Stuffed Joints

Beef joints are not usually stuffed but veal, lamb and pork are frequently boned, stuffed and rolled. Stuffing adds to the flavour of the meat and also makes it go further. The joints should be stuffed, skewered and then securely tied with string. A piece of oiled foil, fixed at the ends of the rolled joint, will prevent the stuffing bursting out during roasting. The string should be removed just before serving, when the meat has cooled a little and set. For stuffing recipes see p. 48-50.

Roast Stuffed Blade of Pork

METRIC
1 blade of pork weighing
approximately 1 ¾ kg
Apple and nut stuffing
(p. 50)
oil for coating
salt
freshly ground pepper

IMPERIAL
1 blade of pork weighing
approximately 3 ½ lb
Apple and nut stuffing
(p. 50)
oil for coating
salt
freshly ground pepper

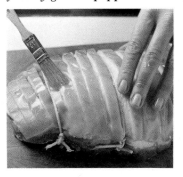

Ask the butcher to bone the joint and to score the skin deeply to make crackling. Pack the stuffing into the cavity where the bone was removed. Secure with skewers and string. Preheat the oven to 220°C, 425°F or gas mark 7. Weigh the stuffed joint and allow 25 minutes per ½ kg/1 lb, plus 25 minutes. Put bones on to make stock for the gravy (p. 14).

Grease a roasting pan, put in the joint, brush all over with oil and sprinkle the skin generously with salt to help crisping. Place in the oven, just above the centre, and cook for 30 minutes or until the skin is golden brown and crispy. Reduce heat to 190°C, 375°F or gas mark 5 and cook for 70 minutes, or until the juice is amber coloured and the crackling is crisp. Pork must NEVER be underdone.

Place the joint on a warm serving dish. Allow the residue to settle in the pan and carefully pour off the fat into a pork dripping pot. Strain in bone stock or use liquor from accompanying vegetables. Scrape up the pan juices and stir over a brisk heat until reduced and a good colour. Season to taste with salt and freshly ground pepper and strain into a warm gravy boat. Serve the pork with Apple sauce (p. 26), Roast potatoes (p. 97) and a fresh green vegetable.

Poultry

Poultry is usually sold ready for cooking, i.e. plucked, drawn and trussed. If frozen the poultry must be thoroughly thawed in the refrigerator or at room temperature for 24 to 48 hours, according to size.

Roast Chicken

When buying chicken, choose a bird weighing about 1¼ kg/2½ lb for two people, 1½ kg/3½ lb for four people, 2 kg/4½ lb for six people.

Method

Clean the giblets and make stock for gravy (p. 14). Preheat the oven to 200°C, 400°F or gas mark 6. Chickens have no external fat so the breast must be protected by covering with fat bacon rashers and well buttered greaseproof paper or foil during roasting, or the flesh will become dry. Prepare the bird and place it in a greased roasting pan in the centre of the oven. Cook for 20 minutes per ½ kg/1 lb. Remove the bacon and paper 20 minutes before the end of the cooking time to allow the breast to brown and crisp. Test by inserting a skewer into the thickest part of the thigh. When the juices run amber coloured, the bird is cooked. Place the chicken on a warm serving dish and make the gravy as for turkey (opposite).

Serve with crisped bacon, roast chipolata sausages and Bread sauce (p. 26), if liked.

Roast Duck and Goose

These birds have a large boney frame so you will need an oven-ready duck weighing 1¾ kg/4 lb for four people, and a 4½ kg/10 lb goose for eight people.

Method

Both birds have a layer of fat beneath the skin of the breast so they do not need covering with bacon or protecting with greaseproof paper or foil. To make the skin crisp, prick the breast all over about 20 minutes before the end of the cooking time. This allows the extra fat to escape into the pan. Fatty birds are best cooked on a grid in the roasting pan with the surplus fat syphoned off from the base of the pan during cooking. Allow the same cooking temperature and time as for chicken, and make the gravy as for turkey (opposite).

Serve with Apple sauce (p. 26) or roast apples, if liked.

Roast Turkey

Turkeys, both fresh and frozen, are now available all year round. They range in size from about 3 kg/6 lb to 10 kg/22 lb. Allow about 350 g/12 oz meat per person. A hen turkey is plumper and more tender than a cock. If frozen the bird must be thoroughly thawed and this takes 36 to 66 hours at room temperature, or until the flesh is soft and no moisture or ice crystals remain in the body cavity. Frozen turkeys are best roasted by the slow method at 160°C, 325°F or gas mark 3. Fresh turkeys which have been hung are best cooked quicker at a higher temperature, 220°C, 425°F or gas mark 7.

Method

Stuff and truss the turkey following the step-by-step instructions. Allow 450 g/1 lb Chestnut or other stuffing (p. 51) for breast of a bird weighing about 7 kg/14 lb. The body cavity of the bird can be filled with Sausage meat stuffing (p. 51). Alternatively chipolata sausages can be baked separately and served around the turkey. Place bird in a greased roasting pan.

Spread softened butter over the turkey and cover the whole of the breast and the top of the legs with fat bacon rashers. Cover the bird with oiled foil and cook for the calculated time — see Guide. About 30 minutes before the end of the cooking time remove the foil and bacon and allow the breast to brown.

Large birds will brown under foil during higher temperature cooking. Meanwhile make Giblet stock (p. 46) for gravy. Test the turkey as for chicken by inserting a skewer into the thigh. When the juice is amber coloured place the bird on a warm serving platter.

To make gravy, carefully pour off the fat from the pan, leaving juices in the bottom. Add the giblet stock, scrape up the juices from the pan and boil briskly until the liquid is reduced and the gravy is a good colour. Season with salt and freshly ground pepper and strain into a warm gravy boat.

Serve the turkey with the crisped bacon, chipolata sausages if used, Bread sauce (p. 26) or cranberry jelly, roast potatoes and Brussels sprouts sautéed with chestnuts (p. 71) if liked.

Stuffed Roast Turkey with Brussels sprouts sautéed with chestnuts and Bread Sauce

Guide To Cooking Times And Servings

STUFFED WEIGHT	APPROX. HOURS AT LOW TEMP	APPROX. HOURS AT HIGH TEMP 200°C, 400°F or gas mark 6	SERVINGS
Capon 3 kg (6 lb)	.....	1½ hours	6-8
Chicken 1½ kg (3½ lb)	.....	1¼ hours	4
Duck 1¾ kg (4 lb)	.....	1¼ hours	4
Goose 4½ kg (10 lb)	.....	2-2¼ hours	6-8
Turkey	160°C, 325°F or gas mark 3	220°C, 425°F or gas mark 7	
2¾-4½ kg (6-10 lb)	3-3¾ hours	2½-2¾ hours	8-12
4½-6½ kg (10-14 lb)	3¾-4¼ hours	2¾-3¼ hours	12-16
6½-7¼ kg (14-16 lb)	4¼-4¾ hours	3¼-3¾ hours	16-20
9-10 kg (20-22 lb)	4¾-5 hours	3¾-4 hours	28-30

Stuffing and Trussing

Oven roasting chicken and turkey is often filled with a savoury stuffing which enhances the flavour, improves the shape and extends the portions (for stuffings see p. 48-50).

Step 1 Draw back the neck flap of the bird and pack some of the stuffing firmly over the breast. Replace the flap and neatly reshape the breast.

Step 2 Turn the bird over, back uppermost. Press the wings against the body and fold the wing tips over onto the flap. Pass a skewer through the right wing, through the end of the flap and through the left wing.

Step 3 Spoon the remaining stuffing through the rear vent into the body of the bird.

Step 4 Turn the chicken over onto its back. Press the thighs against the side of the body, pass a skewer through the bird from one leg to the other. Tie the ends of the drumsticks and the tail stump (parson's nose) neatly together with string.

Step 5 Cover the breast of the chicken with thin de-rinded rashers of fat bacon to protect it from drying. These are removed 20 minutes before the end of the cooking time to allow the breast to brown.

Spit Roasting

This is an excellent method of cooking medium and small joints of roasting meat, poultry and game birds. It has the advantage of visible cooking and it is easier and quicker to clean the back of the grill than the sides of the oven. The meat or poultry on the spit is browned evenly and remains juicy when cold.

It is important that the joint or bird is very neatly trussed and the spit inserted so that the weight is evenly distributed or the joint will slip as it revolves. As meat shrinks during cooking, it may be necessary to re-adjust the forks at either end of the spit and push them more closely into the joint.

Preheat the grill. Brush the joint or bird with oil or melted butter and cook at high heat until it is sealed and golden brown, then reduce the heat and continue cooking until the juice runs amber coloured when tested (except in the case of under-done beef).

Cooking times are the same as for oven roasting: see guides for meat (p. 42) or poultry (p. 45) less 5 minutes per ½ kg/1 lb for unstuffed poultry.

Lean meat and game need basting during cooking but fat joints and chickens are self basting. While the meat is cooking make stock with the bones from the joint (p. 14,16) or use the chicken giblets to make Giblet stock for the gravy. Place the cooked joint or bird on a warm serving plate and remove the skewers and string. Carefully pour the fat from the drip tray, stir in the stock, scraping up the juices from the tray, bring to the boil and reduce until the gravy is a good colour; season and pour into a gravy boat.

Suitable joints for roasting on a spit are *Beef:* boned and rolled rib up to 2 kg/4½ lb. *Veal:* boned and rolled shoulder up to 2 kg/4½ lb. *Lamb:* leg on the bone, whole small leg or fillet or knuckle half. *Pork:* boned and rolled loin and belly up to 2 kg/4½ lb. *Chicken:* 1 up to 2 kg/4½ lb (oven ready weight); 2 broilers (1 kg/2 lb) or 4 poussins (spring chicken).

Giblet Stock

The giblets of oven or spit-roasted chickens can be used to make stock for a gravy or sauce.

The giblets consist of the bird's neck, gizzard (crop) heart and liver. The liver can be reserved for stuffing. Any liver which has been stained yellow by the gall bladder (if broken during drawing) should be cut out and discarded as it will be bitter.

The gizzard should be cut in half, thoroughly washed and all fat removed. Squeeze any blood clots out of the heart and wash under running cold water.

Put the cleaned giblets in a small saucepan, cover with cold water, add a bay leaf, a sprig of parsley, a shallot, 8 peppercorns and ½ teaspoon salt. Cover and simmer for 20 minutes or until required. Strain and use as required.

From the back, left: boned and rolled rib of beef; boned and rolled shoulder of veal; boned and rolled belly of pork; whole small leg of lamb; boned and rolled loin of pork; guineafowl; pheasant; poussin; broiler; duckling; fillet half of leg of lamb; knuckle of lamb

Spit Roasted Chicken with Fresh Herbs

METRIC	IMPERIAL
1 × 1½ kg roasting chicken	1 × 3½ lb roasting chicken
a good bunch of fresh tarragon or chervil	a good bunch of fresh tarragon or chervil
40 g butter	1½ oz butter
1 bay leaf	1 bay leaf
1 sprig parsley	1 sprig parsley
1 shallot or small onion	1 shallot or small onion
salt	salt
black peppercorns	black peppercorns
50 ml white wine (optional)	2 fl oz white wine (optional)
2 tablespoons finely chopped tarragon or chervil leaves	2 tablespoons finely chopped tarragon or chervil leaves
150 ml single cream	¼ pint single cream
lemon juice to taste	lemon juice to taste
TO GARNISH	TO GARNISH
fresh parsley, tarragon or chervil sprigs	fresh parsley, tarragon or chervil sprigs

Truss the chicken, following the instructions on p. 45, but instead of stuffing it, insert several sprigs of fresh tarragon or chervil in the body cavity with a knob of butter. Clean the giblets and put on to cook with water, bay leaf, parsley, shallot, salt and a few black peppercorns to make Giblet stock (opposite).

Heat the grill. Melt the remaining butter and brush it over the chicken. Put the chicken on the spit, with the tray beneath, and grill under high heat for about 20 minutes or until golden. Lower the heat slightly and continue cooking for 50 minutes or until the juice runs amber coloured when tested with a skewer. Baste occasionally with the butter from the drip tray unless the bird is very fatty.

Use only the butter in the drip tray as the juices will stain the chicken if spooned over it. When cooked, place the bird on a warm serving dish. Allow the juices to settle in the drip tray and carefully pour off all the fat. Add the wine (if used) and 150 ml/¼ pint strained giblet stock. Bring to the boil, scraping up the juices from drip tray. Add the tarragon or chervil and the cream. Stir over gentle heat for 5 to 10 minutes and season to taste with salt, pepper and lemon juice. Pour into a warm gravy boat. Serve the chicken garnished with sprigs of fresh parsley, tarragon or chervil and accompany with chips or sauté potatoes and a tossed green salad.

Stuffings and Dumplings

Savoury stuffings, sometimes called forcemeat, add flavour and interest to baked fish and vegetables, roast poultry and meat joints. Dumplings add flavour and interest to soups, stews and casseroles. Stuffing and dumplings are also very useful 'extenders', making a dish more satisfying and stretching it further. Stuffings usually have a base of breadcrumbs, cooked rice or finely minced raw or cooked meat or sausage meat.

English dumplings usually have a suet crust base and are steamed or baked.

Uncooked stuffings containing raw meat or poultry liver should not be frozen.

Mushroom Stuffing; Prune Stuffing; Herb Stuffing

Herb Stuffing
For fish, poultry and meat

METRIC	IMPERIAL
100 g fresh breadcrumbs	*4 oz fresh breadcrumbs*
1 teaspoon dried herbs (see below)	*1 teaspoon dried herbs (see below)*
1 tablespoon chopped parsley	*1 tablespoon chopped parsley*
1 teaspoon grated lemon rind	*1 teaspoon grated lemon rind*
½ teaspoon salt	*½ teaspoon salt*
freshly ground pepper	*freshly ground pepper*
1 small onion, peeled and finely chopped	*1 small onion, peeled and finely chopped*
25 g butter, melted	*1 oz butter, melted*
1 egg, beaten	*1 egg, beaten*
stock or water to bind	*stock or water to bind*

Mix together the breadcrumbs, dried herbs, parsley, lemon rind, salt and pepper to taste. Mix the onion into the breadcrumbs, then stir in the melted butter and beaten egg. Add enough stock or water to bind the mixture and mix thoroughly. Leave the breadcrumbs to swell before using or the stuffing will burst out during cooking. Use sage or savory for duck or goose; lemon thyme for fish, chicken lamb and veal; mint for lamb. Sufficient for 1½ kg (3-3½ lb) shoulder of lamb.

Mushroom Stuffing

For fish, tomatoes, peppers and marrow rings

METRIC	IMPERIAL
50 g streaky bacon or ham, chopped	2 oz streaky bacon or ham, chopped
25 g butter or margarine	1 oz butter or margarine
1 tablespoon finely chopped onion	1 tablespoon finely chopped onion
50 g mushrooms, chopped	2 oz mushrooms, chopped
50 g rice, cooked	2 oz rice, cooked
1 tablespoon chopped parsley	1 tablespoon chopped parsley
or	or
1 teaspoon dried mixed herbs	1 teaspoon dried mixed herbs
salt	salt
pepper	pepper
lemon juice to taste	lemon juice to taste

Cook the bacon over a moderate heat until the fat runs. Add the butter or margarine and fry the onion and mushrooms until softened. Stir in the rice and parsley or dried herbs and season to taste with salt, freshly ground pepper and lemon juice. This is sufficient for 4 four cod steaks.

Prune or Apricot Stuffing

For pork, lamb, chicken, duck, turkey and goose

METRIC	IMPERIAL
50 g butter	2 oz butter
1 onion, peeled and finely chopped	1 onion, peeled and finely chopped
100 g celery, washed and finely chopped	4 oz celery, washed and finely chopped
100 g carrots, scraped and finely chopped	4 oz carrots, scraped and finely chopped
50 g rice, cooked	2 oz rice, cooked
1 tablespoon chopped parsley	1 tablespoon chopped parsley
1 teaspoon paprika pepper	1 teaspoon paprika pepper
salt	salt
freshly ground pepper	freshly ground pepper
lemon juice to taste	lemon juice to taste
50 g prunes or dried apricots, soaked overnight, drained and chopped	2 oz prunes or dried apricots, soaked overnight, drained and chopped

Heat the butter and gently fry the onion and celery until turning golden. Add the carrots, rice and parsley. Mix well and season to taste with paprika pepper, salt and pepper and sharpen with lemon juice. Stir in the prunes or apricots.

This is sufficient for a crown roast of lamb or pork or a guard of honour.

Apple and Nut Stuffing; Sausage Meat Stuffing; Chestnut Stuffing; Rice and Watercress Stuffing

Rice and Watercress Stuffing

For chicken, duck, lamb and veal

METRIC	IMPERIAL
1 bunch watercress	1 bunch watercress
50 g rice, cooked	2 oz rice, cooked
1 tablespoon finely chopped celery	1 tablespoon finely chopped celery
1 tablespoon finely chopped onion	1 tablespoon finely chopped onion
chicken or duck liver (if using for poultry)	chicken or duck liver (if using for poultry)
1 teaspoon salt	1 teaspoon salt
freshly ground pepper	freshly ground pepper
50 g butter, melted	2 oz butter, melted
1 small egg, beaten	1 small egg, beaten

Wash the watercress, discarding any yellow leaves and long stalks, and chop finely. Add it to the rice with the celery and onion. If using liver, clean it, cutting out any discoloured parts, chop and add to the rice. Season to taste. Mix in the melted butter and beaten egg and use immediately. This is sufficient for a large chicken.

Apple and Nut Stuffing

For roast pork, duck and goose

METRIC	IMPERIAL
50 g salted peanuts	2 oz salted peanuts
1 Bramley cooking apple	1 Bramley cooking apple
50 g butter	2 oz butter
1 small onion, finely chopped	1 small onion, finely chopped
2 tablespoons finely chopped celery	2 tablespoons finely chopped celery
50 g fresh breadcrumbs	2 oz fresh breadcrumbs
1 tablespoon chopped parsley	1 tablespoon chopped parsley
1 teaspoon dried savory	1 teaspoon dried savory
salt	salt
freshly ground pepper	freshly ground pepper
lemon juice	lemon juice

Chop the peanuts thoroughly. Peel, core and chop the apple. Heat the butter and fry the peanuts until golden. Add the apple, onion and celery and cook until softened. Stir in the breadcrumbs, parsley and savory. Season well with salt and pepper and lemon juice, to taste. Mix and leave for 20 minutes before using, so that the breadcrumbs can swell. This is sufficient for 1½ kg/3-3½ lb blade of pork.

Sausage Meat Stuffing

For turkey, chicken and veal

METRIC	IMPERIAL
½ kg pork sausage meat	1 lb pork sausage meat
1 medium onion, peeled and finely chopped	1 medium onion, peeled and finely chopped
1 tablespoon chopped parsley	1 tablespoon chopped parsley
1 teaspoon dried mixed herbs	1 teaspoon dried mixed herbs
¼ teaspoon ground mace	¼ teaspoon ground mace
50 g fresh breadcrumbs	2 oz fresh breadcrumbs
salt	salt
freshly ground pepper	freshly ground pepper

Break up the sausage meat with a fork, add the other ingredients with salt and pepper to taste and mix thoroughly. Use to stuff the body cavity of a turkey about 4 kg/9 pounds in weight. For a large chicken use half this quantity, for a boned veal roast adjust quantity according to the size of the joint.

Chestnut Stuffing

For turkey and goose

METRIC	IMPERIAL
50 g streaky bacon	2 oz streaky bacon
25 g butter or margarine	1 oz butter or margarine
turkey or goose liver	turkey or goose liver
1 tablespoon chopped onion	1 tablespoon chopped onion
1 tablespoon chopped celery	1 tablespoon chopped celery
225 g cooked fresh or canned chestnuts, chopped	8 oz cooked fresh or canned chestnuts, chopped
or	or
225 g unsweetened chestnut purée	8 oz unsweetened chestnut purée
50 g fresh breadcrumbs	2 oz fresh breadcrumbs
2 teaspoons grated lemon rind	2 teaspoons grated lemon rind
salt	salt
pepper	pepper
lemon juice to taste	lemon juice to taste
1 egg, beaten	1 egg, beaten

Steamed Suet Dumplings; Herb Dumplings

De-rind and chop the bacon. Cook it gently until the fat runs. Add the butter or margarine and fry the chopped liver, onion and celery until slightly coloured. Stir in the chopped chestnuts or purée. Add the breadcrumbs and lemon rind and mix well. Season to taste with salt and freshly ground pepper and sharpen with lemon juice. Bind with beaten egg. Use to stuff the breast of the bird and put any surplus into the body cavity.

Steamed Suet Dumplings

METRIC	IMPERIAL
100 g plain flour	4 oz plain flour
1½ teaspoons baking powder	1½ teaspoons baking powder
½ teaspoon salt	½ teaspoon salt
50 g shredded suet	2 oz shredded suet
cold water to mix	cold water to mix

Sift the flour with the baking powder and salt. Mix in the suet thoroughly. Add sufficient cold water to make a soft but not sticky dough. On a floured board, shape the dough into a round and divide it into eight pieces. With floured fingers roll each piece into a ball. Drop into boiling salted water or stock, or place on a stew or casserole, cover and simmer gently for 15 minutes, until well risen and fluffy.

Note: Self-raising flour can be used instead of plain flour and baking powder. One tablespoon of chopped fresh parsley may be added to the dry ingredients.

Roast Herb Dumplings

Follow the recipe for Steamed suet dumplings, adding to dry ingredients 1 tablespoon chopped fresh parsley and 1 tablespoon chopped fresh mint for lamb; lemon thyme for veal or chicken; sage or savory for pork or duck. If fresh herbs are not available use 1 teaspoon dried herbs. Mix and shape the dumplings and place them in hot fat round a roasting joint for 20 to 30 minutes before the end of the cooking time; until risen and golden brown. Drain on kitchen paper. Finely chopped onion or grated lemon rind can be added to the dry ingredients for extra flavour.

Pot Roasting: Meat and Poultry

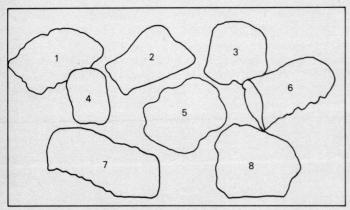

1 Shoulder of lamb, boned and rolled
2 Spare rib joint of pork (forequarter)
3 Beef flank, rolled
4 Breast of lamb, boned and rolled
5 Brisket of beef, rolled
6 Silverside of beef
7 Breast of veal, boned and rolled
8 Beef topside

This is a method of cooking meat joints slowly in a covered flame-proof casserole or thick saucepan. It is very successful with the less tender and cheaper joints such as: *Beef:* topside, silverside, brisket, flank. *Veal:* breast, boned and rolled. *Lamb:* breast and shoulder, boned and rolled. *Pork:* spare rib joint (forequarter).

The joint is first browned quickly in hot fat to seal in the juices. Then a small amount of stock and sometimes wine is added, with a few vegetables, herbs and seasoning. The casserole is tightly covered and the meat is cooked over low heat in its own steam until tender, allowing about 45 minutes per ½ kg/1 pound.

Poultry

Pot roasting is also an excellent way to cook older and less tender fowl, duck and game. The bird should be neatly trussed, as for oven or spit roasting and rubbed over with flour. Fry two chopped de-rinded rashers of bacon gently in a casserole until the fat runs and add 2 tablespoons butter or margarine. When the fat is hot, brown the breast of the bird first on one side and then the other and lastly the front. Turn the bird on to its back, add a glass of wine if liked, a cupful of chicken stock, six button onions, one or two chopped carrots and a stalk of celery. Add a sprig each of parsley and thyme, or tarragon and a bayleaf. Season with salt and freshly ground pepper. Cover tightly and cook over low heat for 2 to 4 hours or until tender, according to the size and age of the bird. Pot roasting of meat and poultry can also be done in a slow oven at 160°C, 325°F or gas mark 3.

Continental Pot Roast of Beef

METRIC
1½ kg piece topside,
  silverside or brisket or
  flank of beef
2 onions
225 g carrots
50 g beef dripping or butter
120 ml red wine
bouquet garni with celery
  (p. 152)
1 teaspoon salt
6-8 peppercorns
beef stock
¾ kg potatoes (optional)

IMPERIAL
3 lb piece topside, silverside
  or brisket or flank of beef
2 onions
8 oz carrots
2 oz beef dripping or butter
4 fl. oz red wine
bouquet garni with celery
  (p. 152)
1 teaspoon salt
6-8 peppercorns
beef stock
1½ lb potatoes (optional)

Step 1 As topside and silverside are very lean, ask the butcher to wrap a piece of larding fat round the joint when trussing it. This is not necessary if using brisket or flank which contain fat and are cheaper cuts.

Peel and quarter the onions, wash and scrape the carrots. Heat the fat in a flameproof casserole and brown the meat quickly all over in the hot fat. Add the onion and carrots and brown lightly.

Step 2 Add the wine, bouquet garni, salt and peppercorns. Cover tightly and cook over a very low heat until tender, about 2 hours. Check the meat occasionally, and if the liquid has evaporated add a little stock as required.

Scraped new potatoes or peeled and quartered old potatoes may be added to the casserole about 1 hour before the end of the cooking time. When cooked, place the meat and vegetables on a warm serving dish. Discard the bouquet garni. Remove the fat from the gravy by drawing kitchen paper across it. Taste and adjust seasoning and strain the gravy into a gravy boat.

Casseroling and Stewing Meat and Poultry

Long, slow cooking in a casserole in a low oven, or in a stewpan on top of the stove, tenderizes and adds flavour to the tougher and cheaper cuts of meat, such as *Beef:* blade, chuck steak. *Veal:* breast, neck, shin or knuckle. *Lamb:* breast, scrag and middle neck. *Pork:* spare rib chops or belly.

Unlike pot roasting, the meat is cut into pieces and cooked completely covered with stock or sauce. For the traditional Irish stew, the lamb is not browned but for beef stews and most casseroles the meat is first browned quickly in hot fat to seal in the juices and the onions and other vegetables are lightly fried to improve the flavour.

Allow 225-350 g/8-12 oz meat per person for stewing veal, lamb or pork on the bone and 175-225 g/6-8 oz for boned meat and stewing steak. The latter usually has a certain amount of fat skin and gristle, which has to be trimmed off and discarded. Casserole dishes reheat very successfully as the flavours mature and are infused into the sauce. They also freeze very well. The casserole or foil container should be kept covered, cooled rapidly and then frozen. They can be defrosted and reheated in one operation in the oven.

A flameproof casserole is ideal for cooking these dishes because the meat and vegetables can be fried in it, the liquid added and the casserole cooked over a low heat on top of the stove or in a slow oven at 160°C, 375°F or gas mark 5, until the meat is tender. Finally the casserole can be put on the dining table and there are no pans to clean.

There are casseroles suitable for dinner parties and hearty ones for family meals.

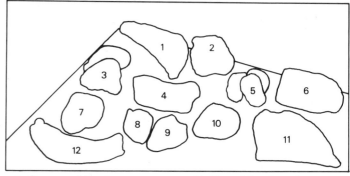

1 *Breast of lamb*
2 *Middle neck of lamb*
3 *Leg of veal*
4 *Chuck steak*
5 *Scrag end of neck of lamb*
6 *Spare rib of pork*
7 *Knuckle of veal*
8 and 9 *Blade of beef*
10 *Beef shin*
11 *Belly of pork*
12 *Breast of veal*

Stewed Steak and Kidney

Although delicious on its own, stewed steak and kidney is traditionally served in a pie, which is illustrated on p. 90.

METRIC	IMPERIAL
¾ kg chuck steak	1 ¾ lb chuck steak
175-225 g ox kidney	6-8 oz ox kidney
2-3 tablespoons flour	2-3 tablespoons flour
50 g lard or beef dripping	2 oz lard or beef dripping
1 tablespoon chopped onion	1 tablespoon chopped onion
stock or water to cover	stock or water to cover
salt	salt
freshly ground pepper	freshly ground pepper

Cut the steak into 3½ cm/1½ inch cubes, removing any fat and gristle. Cut the kidney into smaller chunks than the meat, discarding the fatty core. Toss the steak and kidney in flour in a paper bag. Shake off any surplus flour. Fry the onion in hot lard or beef dripping in a sauté pan until transparent. Add the steak and kidney and fry, stirring, until nicely browned. Cover with stock or water and season with salt and freshly ground pepper to taste.

Bring to the simmer and cook very gently on top of the stove or in a slow oven until the meat is tender, about 1½ to 2 hours.

For pie filling, allow the meat to cool and skim off the fat.

Flemish Carbonade of Beef

METRIC	IMPERIAL
¾ kg top rump or chuck steak, cut into thin slices	1 ½ lb top rump or chuck steak, cut into thin slices
50 g lard	2 oz lard
225 g onions, peeled and sliced	8 oz onions, peeled and sliced
100 g mushrooms, washed and sliced	4 oz mushrooms, washed and sliced
2-3 tablespoons flour	2-3 tablespoons flour
2 teaspoons brown sugar	2 teaspoons brown sugar
300 ml brown ale	½ pint brown ale
beef stock as required	beef stock as required
salt	salt
freshly ground pepper	freshly ground pepper
bouquet garni	bouquet garni
40-50 g butter	1 ½-2 oz butter
6 thick slices French bread	6 thick slices French bread
continental mustard	continental mustard
TO GARNISH	TO GARNISH
parsley sprigs	parsley sprigs

Cut the beef into strips about 3½-5 cm/1½-2 inches wide. Heat the lard and quickly fry the slices of beef until brown on both sides, then remove them from the casserole. Add the onions and mushrooms and fry until the onions are transparent. Remove the casserole from the heat and stir in sufficient flour to absorb the lard and add the sugar.

Return the casserole to the heat and fry the flour, stirring, until the roux is caramel coloured. Reduce the heat and gradually stir in the ale. Bring to the boil, add the steak and sufficient stock to cover. Season to taste with salt and freshly ground pepper and add the bouquet garni. Cover and cook in the centre of preheated oven at 170°C, 325°F or gas mark 3 for 1½ hours. Remove the bouquet garni.

Spread butter on one side of the bread slices and mustard on the other. Arrange the slices, butter side uppermost, on top of the meat. Continue cooking for 20 to 30 minutes on the top shelf of the oven until the meat is tender and the bread has soaked up the gravy underneath and become crusty on top.

Garnish with parsley and serve with Brussels sprouts or green beans.

Normandy Chicken with Apple and Cider

METRIC	IMPERIAL
1 oven-ready chicken, about 1½ kg	*1 oven-ready chicken, about 3½ lb*
chicken giblets	*chicken giblets*
1 bay leaf	*1 bay leaf*
1 sprig parsley	*1 sprig parsley*
8 peppercorns	*8 peppercorns*
½ teaspoon salt	*½ teaspoon salt*
approx. 50 g flour	*approx. 2 oz flour*
50 g unsalted butter or lard	*2 oz unsalted butter or lard*
1 large onion, peeled and sliced	*1 large onion, peeled and sliced*
1-2 stalks celery, washed and chopped	*1-2 stalks celery, washed and chopped*
1 large or 2 small cooking apples, peeled and chopped	*1 large or 2 small cooking apples, peeled and chopped*
150 ml dry cider	*¼ pint dry cider*
4 tablespoons double cream	*4 tablespoons double cream*
salt	*salt*
freshly ground pepper	*freshly ground pepper*
TO GARNISH	TO GARNISH
1 dessert apple	*1 dessert apple*
25 g butter	*1 oz butter*
celery leaves	*celery leaves*

Joint the chicken as described on the facing page. Skin the joints by holding the narrow end firmly with the left hand and drawing the skin upwards and off with the right hand. Use a damp cloth to hold both the joint and the skin as both are greasy and tend to slip. Put the skin, carcass, giblets, herbs and peppercorns and salt in a saucepan, cover with cold water and make Giblet stock (p. 46).

Coat the chicken joints with flour; pat off surplus and reserve it. Heat the butter or lard in a flameproof casserole and fry the joints until golden brown all over, then remove them from the casserole. Gently fry the onion and celery until they are softened. Add the apple and cook for 5 minutes.

Draw the casserole off the heat, stir in sufficient flour (about 3 tablespoons) to absorb the fat. Gradually stir in the cider and 300 ml/½ pint strained giblet stock. Bring to the simmer, replace the chicken joints in the casserole and add more giblet stock if necessary to cover the chicken. Put the lid on the casserole and cook over gentle heat for 30 minutes or until the chicken legs are tender. Remove the chicken and boil the sauce briskly without a lid until it has thickened slightly. Mix 3 tablespoons of the sauce into the cream and stir the mixture into the casserole. Taste and adjust the seasoning. Replace the chicken.

Core the unpeeled dessert apple and cut it into rings. Fry the rings in the butter until golden brown on each side and arrange them on top of the chicken with little tufts of fresh celery leaves. Serve with boiled or creamed potatoes and buttered peas, green beans or broccoli.

Jointing a Chicken

Chicken should be divided into portions before it is made into a casserole. If it is jointed neatly, one bird will make two meals; the legs and breasts can be used for the casserole and the carcass and giblets for a good stock. The meat from the boiled carcass and giblets can be used for a savoury risotto or pasta dish or as a filling for vol-au-vents.

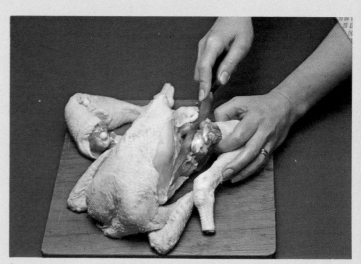

Step 1 Insert a sharp knife between right thigh and body of bird and cut through the skin (but not flesh) to thigh joint. *Push* thigh upwards until joint is dislocated. With the point of the knife, cut through between ball and socket. If jointing a large bird (1¾ kg/4 lb or over) separate thigh and drumstick by dislocating the joint and cutting between ball and socket in same way. Repeat with left leg.

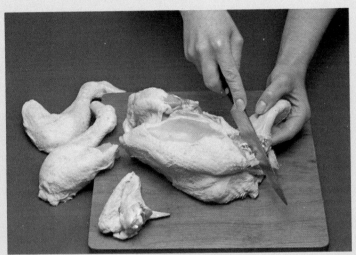

Step 2 Cut down to the joint where the right wing joins the body, keeping as close to the joint as possible, and leaving the breast intact. Insert the knife between the ball and socket and sever the wing. Cut off the wing tips, which are boney, and use them for stock. Repeat with the left wing.

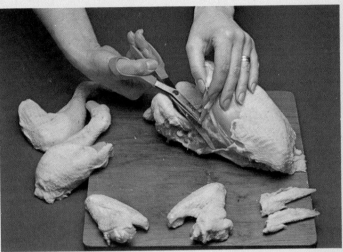

Step 3 If the bird is large, slice off part of the breast behind the wishbone. If jointing a bird 1½ kg/3½ lb or smaller, leave the breast intact. Use kitchen scissors or poultry shears to cut along the bottom of the rib cage on each side of breast and separate it from the back by dislocating the front bones.

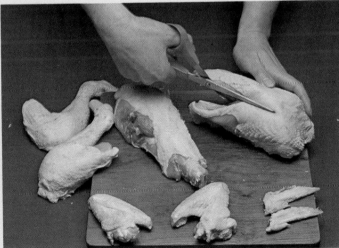

Step 4 Divide the breast into two by cutting along one side of the breast bone with a knife or shears. If preferred, the breast can be filleted off each side of the breastbone.

Frying   Shallow Frying: Meat, Liver, Kidney, Bacon

This popular, quick way of cooking meat is suitable only for tender prime cuts, the same as those chosen for grilling (p. 38). The cooking time is also similar.

Calves', lambs' and pork liver and kidney should be sliced, and the fatty core of the kidney removed (p. 39). Cook quickly, as offal becomes hard if overcooked. Calves' liver is the most delicate and the most expensive; ox liver is the cheapest but is not suitable for frying.

Trim the meat, removing surplus fat and skin. Coat with flour, shaking off any surplus flour which may fall into the fat and burn. Alternatively, coat with egg and breadcrumbs (p. 62).

To fry

Heat the fat, oil, butter or lard in a thick frying pan. Use just enough to cover the base of the pan. Fry the meat briskly, first on one side and then the other. This will be sufficient for under-done steak, entrecôtes and escalopes. For well-done steak, chops and cutlets, turn down the heat and continue cooking until tender, turning once.

When cooked, place the meat on a warm serving dish and make the gravy, if liked.

Deglazing the pan and making gravy

Pour into the frying pan a glass of wine and/or stock. Use red wine or dry sherry for beef, pork and lamb; white wine or dry vermouth for veal; sherry or Marsala for pork. Boil briskly, scraping up the juices from the base of the pan until the gravy is a good colour, and season to taste. For a richer gravy, stir in 2 or 3 tablespoons single cream. Pour the gravy over the meat and serve immediately.

Sausages

Fry beef and pork sausages slowly or the skin may burst. Turn them frequently so that they brown evenly.

Bacon rashers

Stretch bacon rashers with the back of a knife and cut off the rind and any gristle (p. 39). Heat the rashers slowly without any extra fat until the bacon fat is transparent. If crispy bacon is wanted cook for longer. Back rashers are the finest and most expensive, collar (shoulder) is leaner and coarser. Streaky rashers from the belly of pork are the least expensive; they are very sweet and crisp up well. Green bacon is mild-cured, smoked bacon has a stronger flavour and is sometimes salty.

Bacon cuts suitable for shallow frying, clockwise from the back: streaky; collar; two cuts of unsmoked back.

Fried liver and bacon

METRIC	IMPERIAL
½ kg sliced calves' or lamb's liver	1 lb sliced calves' or lamb's liver
8 bacon rashers, back or streaky	8 bacon rashers, back or streaky
4 tomatoes	4 tomatoes
salt	salt
freshly ground pepper	freshly ground pepper
50 g lard or cooking fat	2 oz lard or cooking fat
1 tablespoon chopped onion	1 tablespoon chopped onion
120 ml red or white wine or stock	4 fl oz red or white wine or stock
parsley sprigs to garnish	parsley sprigs to garnish

Step 1 Cut out any gristle from the liver and coat with flour, shaking off any surplus. Stretch the bacon rashers with back of a knife and cut off the rind and gristle. Halve the tomatoes crosswise, not down, and season with salt and pepper.

Step 2 Arrange the bacon rashers in a frying pan and heat slowly until nicely crisped. Remove to a warm serving dish. Add the lard or fat to the pan, heat it and fry the tomatoes quickly, first outside and then cut side, until they begin to go golden. Place them on the serving dish.

Step 3 Put in the liver slices carefully to avoid splashing. Fry briskly until crisp underneath, turn and fry the other side. Do not overcook or the liver will be hard. Remove to the serving dish. Add the chopped onion to the fat and fry, stirring, until it begins to change colour.

Pour in the wine or stock and bring to the boil, scraping up the juices from the bottom of the pan. Add a little extra stock or water if needed. Season to taste with salt and pepper. Arrange the liver slices overlapping on serving dish with bacon rashers. Pour the hot gravy over the liver and garnish with the tomatoes and parsley.

Shallow Frying: Fish

Fish suitable for shallow frying are small round fish weighing 175-350 g/6-12 oz, such as trout and whiting; flat fish such as plaice, lemon sole, Dover sole, witches, flounder and brill; and fillets of large white fish such as whiting, haddock, cod and mock halibut (monkfish).

Round Fish

These are not usually skinned but are scaled (p. 40) if necessary. The head and tail are usually left on but the fins are trimmed.

To gut round fish, slit the belly from the gills down to the vent just above the tail. Scrape out the entrails onto waste paper so they may be easily discarded. Wash the cavity thoroughly under running cold water. Dry the fish with absorbent kitchen paper.

Flat Fish

These are usually skinned, (p. 40) but sometimes only the dark skin is removed. The head and tail are left on. To gut flat fish, cut a slit on the dark skin side just below the head and scrape out the entrails. Wash the cavity thoroughly under running cold water. Dry the fish with absorbent kitchen paper.

To Fry

Butter is the best fat to choose for frying fish because it imparts its flavour to the fish. Use clarified butter for frying as butter will burn unless it is first clarified (p. 153). Coat round or flat fish or fillets with flour and shake off any surplus. Heat sufficient clarified butter to cover base of a frying pan and fry the fish for about 5 minutes on each side, turning once only. Fish fillets should be golden brown and whole fish should be cooked until the flesh shrinks away from the bone at the head end. Keep the fish warm while you deglaze the pan. Add 1 tablespoon of butter to the pan and heat it. Stir in 1 to 2 tablespoons of chopped fresh parsley or chervil and fry for a minute or two until it is bright green. Add the juice of half a lemon or a small glass of dry white wine and bring it to the boil. Arrange the fish on a warm serving dish and pour the sauce over it. Garnish with lemon wedges and parsley sprigs. Serve immediately. Fish fried meunière style loses its crispness and becomes greasy if it is kept waiting.

Trout Meunière with Almonds

Meunière means in the style of the miller's wife, i.e. the trout are fished out of the millstream, cooked and served as quickly as possible while still sparkling fresh.

From the back, flat fish: left, Dover sole; right, lemon sole; left, plaice; right, flounder. Fish fillets; monkfish; haddock; cod. Small round fish: whiting, trout.

METRIC	IMPERIAL
4 trout, weighing 225-350 g each	4 trout, weighing 8-12 oz each
flour for coating	flour for coating
175 g clarified butter (p. 153)	6 oz clarified butter (p. 153)
6 tablespoons flaked almonds	6 tablespoons flaked almonds
4-5 tablespoons lemon juice or dry white wine	4-5 tablespoons lemon juice or dry white wine
salt	salt
freshly ground pepper	freshly ground pepper
TO GARNISH	TO GARNISH
lemon wedges	lemon wedges
parsley sprigs	parsley sprigs

Scale and gut the trout as described for round fish on p. 40 and on facing page. Remove the eyes from the head. Dry the fish and coat evenly with flour, shaking off any surplus. Heat 50 g/2 oz clarified butter in a frying pan until very hot. Put in the trout and fry quickly until golden brown underneath.

Turn the fish carefully, using a fish slice and palette knife, so as not to break the skin, and fry the other side. Cook until the second side is crisp and the flesh shrinks away from the backbone just below the head. Lift the fish onto a heated serving dish and keep it warm. Add the remaining clarified butter to the pan, heat it and fry the flaked almonds until golden. Add the lemon juice or wine and season with salt and pepper to taste. Bring to the boil and pour the sauce and almonds over the fish. Garnish with lemon wedges and parsley sprigs. Serve immediately with new potatoes, boiled and tossed in butter and chopped parsley, or Sauté potatoes (p. 70).

Variation

Aux champignons; in place of the almonds, add 100 g/4 oz sliced button mushrooms, fried in butter.

Shallow Frying: Coating with Egg and Breadcrumbs

Fish fillets, fish cakes, veal escalopes and lamb cutlets are particularly good when coated with egg and breadcrumbs and fried in shallow fat – either lard, cooking oil or clarified butter. It is not difficult if you remember the following points:

1. Do the coating well in advance so the egg can harden and the crumbs will not fall off during cooking.
2. Be sure the fat is sizzling hot so the coating will be crisp and golden. If the fat is not hot enough at the start, the food will be greasy and a poor colour.
3. When cooking fish or meat in batches, strain the fat between each frying and wipe out the pan with absorbent kitchen paper or burnt breadcrumbs will get on the food.
4. After frying, spread the fried fish or meat on absorbent kitchen paper to drain and keep warm. Do not pile portions on top of each other.
5. If reheating the fish, put it in a preheated oven for 10 minutes. To freeze, wrap portions individually. Defrost and reheat the frozen fish in the oven in one operation.   You can use a whole egg or an egg yolk beaten with a teaspoon of water for coating.

White breadcrumbs, freshly made in a blender, give the most even colour when fried, but dried crumbs are very good and can be stored without going mouldy. Bake surplus crusts in a low oven until crisp and crush with a rolling pin or put in a blender. Alternatively you can buy ready-made crumbs. The fine crumbs are best for frying, the coarser 'country crumbs' are better for topping oven and gratin dishes.

Escalopes of Veal Viennoise

Allow 1 veal escalope, weighing about 100 g/4 oz per person. Put the escalope between sheets of greaseproof paper and beat it with a rolling pin until it is thin. Coat with flour and fry as for fillets of fish (see step-by-step pictures).

Garnish with chopped hard-boiled eggs, anchovy fillets, capers and lemon wedges. If liked, serve with Tartare sauce (p. 28) and Sauté potatoes, (p. 70).

Escalopes of Veal Viennoise with Sauté Potatoes and Tartare Sauce

Fried fillets of fish

Suitable fish are plaice, lemon sole, witches, monkfish, whiting, haddock, codling. Allow about 175 g/6 oz filleted fish per person, either 2 small fillets or 1 large fillet, this is easier to handle if cut across in half. For filleting instructions see p. 150.

Step 1 Trim and wash the fillets. Dry with absorbent kitchen paper. Coat evenly with flour and shake off any surplus. Beat an egg until liquid and pour it into a shallow dish. Spread a thick bed of crumbs on a sheet of greaseproof paper. Coat the fillets one at a time. Lay each fillet skinless side down in the egg. Hold the tail and brush egg over the top side.

Step 2 Draw the fillet out over the side of the dish to remove surplus egg, allowing the egg to drip back into the dish, not into the crumbs.

Step 3 Lay the fillet skinless side down on the bed of crumbs. Use the edges of the paper to toss more crumbs over the top of the fish. Sprinkle on more crumbs when necessary.

Step 4 Press the fillet down firmly into the bed of crumbs with the heel of your hand. Lift it by the tail, shake off loose crumbs and lay it face upwards to harden so the coating will remain firm while frying.

Step 5 Heat sufficient cooking fat to cover completely the base of the frying pan. When the fat hazes or the oil starts to seeth, carefully put in the fillets, skinless side down first and fry until golden underneath. Turn carefully with a fish slice and palette knife and fry the other side. Drain on absorbent kitchen paper and keep warm.

Step 6 Arrange the fillets, best side upwards, overlapping on a warm serving plate. Garnish with lemon butterflies and parsley sprigs. Serve with Tartare sauce (p. 28) if liked.

Crispy Herrings in Oatmeal

METRIC
4 herrings weighing about
275-350 g each
milk
medium oatmeal for coating
175 g butter

TO GARNISH
lemon wedges
parsley sprigs

IMPERIAL
4 herrings weighing about
10-12 oz each
milk
medium oatmeal for coating
6 oz butter

TO GARNISH
lemon wedges
parsley sprigs

Step 1 Scale and clean as for round fish (p. 60) slitting the belly right down to the tail. Cut off head, fins and tail. Open out flat and place, skin side uppermost, on a board. Press firmly with knuckles all along backbone to loosen it.

Step 2 Turn the herring over and with the point of a knife ease out the backbone in one piece, starting at the head end. Remove as many of the small bones as possible. Wash the fish and dry with kitchen paper.

Step 3 Dip fish in milk, coat with oatmeal following the method for egg and breadcrumbs (p. 62). Fry in hot butter, skinless side first, until crisp, then turn and fry other side. Drain on kitchen paper. If the herring has roe, coat and fry it separately and place down centre of each fish. Garnish with lemon wedges and parsley sprigs. Serve hot with Gooseberry sauce (p. 27) or Mustard sauce (p. 23) if liked.

Dressed Lamb Cutlets

METRIC	IMPERIAL
8 neck cutlets of lamb	8 neck cutlets of lamb
beaten egg and breadcrumbs for coating	beaten egg and breadcrumbs for coating
lard or clarified butter for frying	lard or clarified butter for frying
1 kg creamy Mashed potatoes (p. 98)	2 lb creamy Mashed potatoes (p. 98)
TO GARNISH	TO GARNISH
fresh mint or parsley sprigs	fresh mint or parsley sprigs

Step 1 Remove the chine bone from the chops and trim off the surplus fat. Cut 2.5 cm/1 inch of meat off the ends of the rib bones and scrape the bones clean.

Step 2 Coat the chops with egg and crumbs (p. 62) and leave the coating to harden. Fry in hot fat for 5 minutes on each side, turning once. Drain on kitchen paper.

Step 3 Make a mound of creamy mashed potatoes in the centre of a warm serving platter and mark in it a pattern with a fork or spoon handle. Put a cutlet frill on the end of each cutlet bone and stand the cutlets round the potatoes with the frills in the centre. Garnish with sprigs of fresh mint or parsley. Serve with Cumberland sauce (p. 26) or Tartare sauce (p. 28) if liked.

Crispy Herrings in Oatmeal

Deep Frying

For deep frying, the food is totally immersed in the hot fat. A deep pan with a thick base and a frying basket are needed and sufficient fat to fill the pan half or two-thirds full. You will need about 1-1½ kg/2¼-3 lb solid fat or 1½ litres/2½ pints cooking oil. There must always be considerable space above the suface of the fat to allow it to rise when the food is put in or the fat might overflow and catch alight.

Safety Tips

Never drag a pan of fat across the top of a hot stove. Always lift a pan carefully from one place to another. Should the fat ever catch alight, NEVER try to use water to put it out as it will only splash burning fat around. Turn off the gas or electricity and cover the pan with the lid. The flames will quickly go out when the oxygen is excluded.

Suitable Fats and Storage

The fats to use are lard or solid vegetable fats, clarified dripping or cooking oil. They must be clear and free from moisture or they will spit when heating and not rise to the right temperature.

After frying, cool the fat and strain it through a fine sieve into a bowl or wide-mouthed jar and keep it covered. Do not mix solid fat and oil. Clean fat can be stored and used repeatedly, so it is very economical. Top it up with fresh fat when necessary.

Frying Temperatures

As with shallow frying, the temperature of the fat is vital – if the temperature is too low the food will be grease-sodden. If it is too hot, the food will burn before it is cooked through. When solid fat produces a slight haze, it is hot enough. Oil should just seeth; if it smokes it is too hot. A fat thermometer, which is clearly marked is the best way to check the temperature. Put it in as you heat the fat and read it at eye level to be accurate.

Remember that putting cold food into hot fat will lower the temperature to start with, but that temperature will go on rising after the food is cooked, unless the heat is reduced. Adjust the temperature between each batch of frying. If you have no thermometer, use a bread cube to test the temperature. If it sinks, the fat is not hot enough. If it rises and becomes crisp in 20 seconds, it is the right temperature for most foods to start frying – 190°C, 375°F.

If the food is fairly thick, such as fish fillets in batter or Scotch eggs, and needs time to cook through, start frying at a lower temperature (163°C, 325°F) when a cube of bread will take about 60 seconds to brown.

When the fat is at the right temperature it seals the surface of the food and prevents the flavour of the food escaping into the fat and the food itself will be crisp and non greasy.

French Fried Onions Rings; Chips; Matchstick Potatoes; Crinkle-cut Chips; Fried Parsley

French Fried Onion Rings

Skin a large Spanish onion and cut into 5 mm/¼ inch slices. Separate the slices into rings. Dip the rings in milk and toss them in seasoned flour, shaking off any surplus. Heat deep fat to 190°C, 375°F. Put the onion rings in a heated frying basket (facing page) and cook for 2 to 3 minutes until crisp and golden. Drain on absorbent kitchen paper sprinkle with salt and serve at once with grilled or fried fish or meat.

Fried Parsley

This is a pretty and deliciously crisp garnish for fried and grilled dishes.

Remove long stalks from the parsley, wash and dry the sprigs. Cook in deep fat at 182°C, 360°F for about 2 minutes. As soon as the parsley starts sizzling remove it with a slotted spoon. Drain on absorbent kitchen paper and use at once.

Chipped Potatoes

To make sure chipped potatoes are served really crisp and golden they must be fried twice. The first frying gets rid of the excess water in the potatoes and is called BLANCHING; it can be done well in advance of the meal. The second frying takes only 1 to 2 minutes in the hot fat or oil and should be done just before serving. Allow 225 g/8 oz medium to large potatoes for each serving. For general use, cut the chips about 1 cm/½ inch thick with a knife or wavy cutter; for poultry and game cut them thinner and shorter, these are called straws or matchstick potatoes. The latter cook very quickly in the second frying.

Step 1 Peel and wash the potatoes. Cut into slices 1 cm/½ inch thick, then into strips of the same thickness. The ends can be squared off and trimmings used for soup. Dry chips in clean cloth and keep covered or they will discolour. If kept in cold water they tend to lose vitamin C.

Step 2 Fill a deep frying pan two-thirds full with oil or fat. Put in the frying basket and heat it in the oil or the food will stick to it when frying. Heat the oil or fat to 182°C, 360°F. Remove basket, put in a thick layer of chips and slowly lower it into the pan. Cook for 3 to 4 minutes or until chips are tender but not brown. Lift out basket, allowing fat to drain back into pan. Spread chips on kitchen paper to drain. Reheat oil or fat between batches.

Step 3 Just before the chips are required, reheat the fat to 190°C, 375°F. Put the first batch of chips in the basket and fry for 1 to 2 minutes or until crisp and golden. Remove the basket, drain the fat back into the pan. Spread the chips on absorbent kitchen paper to drain, sprinkle with salt and serve very hot as soon as possible.

Sauté Meat

The French word sauté has been adopted into the English language, and this method of cooking is popular in English kitchens.

The meat is cut into fairly small pieces and fried quickly in hot fat. Chopped onions or mushrooms may then be added and fried lightly. A little liquid is then added to the pan and the cooking is completed in 10 to 20 minutes over gentle heat. The sauce is not usually thickened, so there is no need to make a roux, and you have a tasty dish in minimum time.

This is very convenient, but it does mean you have to choose meat which will be tender when cooked quickly, such as well-hung rump steak, entrecôte, fillet of beef, lamb, pork or veal, liver and kidneys. Sliced chicken breast is also suitable.

When the meat is nicely browned, red or white wine, sherry, Marsala or vermouth is usually added to deglaze the pan (see step 3) then stock or cream is added with herbs and seasoning. This is simmered gently and as soon as the meat is tender, the dish is served with rice, pasta or potatoes and selected vegetables.

For large amounts it is best to use a sauté pan, which is deeper than a frying pan and has straight sides and a lid. For small quantities use a skillet, i.e. a frying pan with a lid, or a chafing dish — a copper pan designed for use with a spirit stove for quick cooking in the dining room, on the table or sideboard.

Pork Fillet with Mushrooms and Soured Cream

METRIC	IMPERIAL
½ kg pork fillet	1¼ lb pork fillet
2-3 tablespoons flour	2-3 tablespoons flour
100-175 g button mushrooms	4-6 oz button mushrooms
50 g lard or unsalted butter	2 oz lard or unsalted butter
2 tablespoons sherry or vermouth	2 tablespoons sherry or vermouth
150 ml soured cream	¼ pint soured cream
¼ teaspoon dried savory or mixed herbs	¼ teaspoon dried savory or mixed herbs
salt	salt
freshly ground pepper	freshly ground pepper
250 ml stock or bouillon	8 fl oz stock or bouillon
cooked rice or Duchess potatoes to serve	cooked rice or Duchess potatoes to serve
TO GARNISH	TO GARNISH
fried mushroom caps	fried mushroom caps
paprika pepper or chopped parsley	paprika pepper or chopped parsley

Step 1 Trim any fat or skin from the fillet and cut the meat across into slices about 2.5 cm/1 inch thick. Flatten the slices slightly with a rolling pin. Coat with flour, shaking off any surplus. Trim off the mushroom stalks, rinse the caps under cold running water and dry on absorbent kitchen paper.

Step 2 Heat the lard or butter in a sauté pan; when a slight haze rises from the fat, add the pork slices in a single layer. Fry briskly until crisp underneath, turn and fry the other side. Add the mushrooms and cook for 5 minutes, shaking the pan frequently.

Step 3 Pour in the sherry or vermouth and bubble up, scraping up the juices from the bottom of the pan: this is called deglazing. Cook gently for a minute or two.

Step 4 Lower the heat and stir in the soured cream. Add the herbs, salt and pepper to taste and mix well. Stir in sufficient stock to just cover the pork. Cook gently for 5-10 minutes or until the pork is tender. Taste and adjust the seasoning as necessary.

Make a border of cooked rice or Duchess potatoes (p. 98) and spoon in the pork and sauce. Garnish with fried mushroom caps and paprika or chopped parsley. Note: As an alternative to soured cream, stir 2 tablespoons of lemon juice into 150 ml/¼ pint double cream. If using a bouillon cube instead of stock, remember it is salty, so taste and adjust the seasoning as necessary.

Sauté Vegetables

This is a much more interesting way of cooking vegetables than boiling.

Root vegetables such as carrots, turnips, parsnips and potatoes and also sprouts, need to be par-boiled before they are sautéed. Aubergines, courgettes, cucumber, mushrooms, sliced onions, peppers and cabbage can be put raw into the hot pan, sautéed in butter and flavoured with herbs, preferably fresh. Unlike sauté meat, no liquid is added to the pan during cooking.

Sauté Potatoes

METRIC	IMPERIAL
¾ kg small or medium potatoes	1½ lb small or medium potatoes
50 g butter or lard	2 oz butter or lard
salt	salt
freshly ground pepper	freshly ground pepper
TO GARNISH	TO GARNISH
chopped chives or parsley	chopped chives or parsley

Step 1 Scrub the potatoes and boil them in well salted water for 10 minutes or until they begin to get tender. Do not cook the potatoes completely or they will fall to pieces in the sauté pan. Drain in a colander and cool slightly. Peel them and cut into 5 mm/¼ inch thick slices.

Step 2 Heat the butter or lard in a large frying pan with a thick base. Spread the potatoes in a single layer over the bottom of the pan and fry until golden brown underneath. Using a palette knife, turn slices and fry the other side. Sauté potatoes in batches if necessary; do not crowd the pan.

Step 3 Spread the potatoes on absorbent kitchen paper to drain. Sprinkle with salt and pepper. Keep hot in a warm oven while frying the next batch. Serve the sauté potatoes in a hot vegetable dish. Garnish with chopped parsley or chives.

Carrots, Turnips, Parsnips

Choose small, preferably young vegetables. Peel, wash and cut them into slices about 5 mm/¼ inch thick. Drop them into boiling water and cook for 10 minutes or until slightly softened. Do not cook until tender or the slices will break up in the sauté pan. Drain thoroughly in a colander and spread on a clean cloth or absorbent kitchen paper to dry.

For ½ kg/1 lb of vegetables, heat 50 g/2 oz butter in a sauté pan, skillet or frying pan. Use a pan large enough for the sliced vegetables to be spread over the base. Cook gently for 5 to 10 minutes, shaking the pan frequently – stirring tends to break up the slices. Turn the vegetables with a fish slice and fry the other side. Sprinkle with 2 tablespoons chopped fresh mint (particularly good with carrots) tarragon, chervil or parsley. Serve hot as soon as possible.

A selection of sauté vegetables, from the back: Brussels sprouts; carrots; potatoes; courgettes; onions; cabbage; peppers

Brussels Sprouts

Choose small tight sprouts. Trim off the stalks and remove any discoloured leaves. Cook in boiling salted water for 10 minutes and drain thoroughly. For ½ kg/1 lb sprouts, heat 50 g/2 oz butter and sauté the sprouts until they begin to turn golden. Season well with freshly ground pepper and a little ground nutmeg.

Brussels Sprouts with Chestnuts

Add 225 g/8 oz freshly boiled and peeled or canned chestnuts to the sprouts and sauté together and season with salt, freshly ground pepper and a pinch of ground nutmeg. This is good with roast turkey, duck, goose and game.

Aubergines, Courgettes, Cucumbers

Wipe the vegetables and remove the stalks. Cucumber may be peeled if preferred. Slice them about 5 mm/¼ inch thick. Spread the slices on a clean cloth and sprinkle with salt. Leave for excess water to be extracted – it is exuded in little bubbles on the surface. Rinse off the salt under cold water and dry. Sauté as for carrots; aubergines may need a little more butter. Flavour with lemon thyme or basil; if using dried herbs, 1 teaspoon will be sufficient.

Onions

Peel, thinly slice and sauté in butter or lard. Cook over gentle heat, shaking the pan frequently, until the onions are softened and slightly coloured. Season and garnish with chopped parsley.

Peppers

Wipe peppers and slice thinly, discarding membrane and seeds. Sauté as for onion until tender, season with salt.

Cabbage

Remove tough outer leaves, quarter the cabbage and remove the stalk. Slice thinly, rinse in cold water and dry well. Sauté as for onions, stirring from time to time. Do not overcook; it is better slightly crisp. Season with salt, freshly ground pepper and a little ground nutmeg.

Simmering Meat Joints and Poultry

This method of cooking joints is usually done on top of the stove, but it can also be done in a slow oven at 150°C, 300°F or gas mark 2. It is often called boiled meat, but the temperature must be carefully controlled and the water should be kept just below boiling point, i.e. 96°C, 205°F. It must be just moving, but with no large bubbles. Hard boiling makes the meat tough. Simmering is excellent for the tough, less expensive joints such as fresh or salt brisket of beef, pickled belly of pork, forehock of bacon and boiling fowl, as well as the choice cuts such as fresh or salted silverside of beef, ox tongue, leg of mutton, gammon and ham.

Joints and birds should be neatly trussed and tied with string before cooking. Smoked gammon and ham should be soaked in cold water – 4 hours for mild-cured joints, overnight if salty.

Put the meat in a large pan, cover with cold water and bring slowly to the boil. Lower the heat, skim off any scum, add some prepared root vegetables, a bay leaf, parsley, a few peppercorns and salt (unless the meat is pickled or cured). Cover tightly and simmer very gently for about 30 minutes per ½ kg/1 lb and 30 minutes over. The exact time depends on the cut and quality of the meat or the age of the fowl. If adding vegetables to serve with the joint, put them in the pan 1 hour before the end of the estimated cooking time.

Gammon joints suitable for simmering, from the back, clockwise (right): corner gammon; middle gammon; gammon slipper; hock, boned and rolled

Serving Suggestions

Beef
Serve hot with mixed root vegetables and boiled potatoes, garnished with chopped parsley, Steamed suet dumplings, (p. 51) horseradish cream or mustard.

Serve cold with Baked jacket potatoes (p. 99) or Potato salad (p. 112) and pickles.

Boiled Leg of Mutton
Serve hot with Mashed potatoes or swedes (p. 98) and Caper sauce (p. 23).

Serve cold with hot Potato salad (p. 112) and chutney.

Boiled Pickled Belly of Pork
Serve hot with Pease pudding (p. 111) or Butter beans in Parsley sauce (p. 110).

Serve cold with pickles and Coleslaw (p. 113).

Boiled Ham or Gammon
Serve hot with Stuffed baked potatoes (p. 99), buttered spinach and Cumberland sauce (p. 26).

Serve cold with Maitre d'hôtel potatoes (p. 97) or Rosy winter salad (p. 112).

Boiled Fowl
Serve hot with boiled rice and leeks in Cheese sauce (p. 23) made with chicken stock.

Serve cold with mixed salads and Mayonnaise or Mousseline sauce (p. 29).

Boiled Brisket of Beef and Dumplings

METRIC	IMPERIAL
1½ kg salted brisket of beef or silverside	3 lb salted brisket of beef or silverside
bouquet garni (p. 152)	bouquet garni (p. 152)
3-4 medium onions, peeled	3-4 medium onions, peeled
225 g carrots, scraped and sliced	8 oz carrots, scraped and sliced
1 medium turnip, peeled and quartered	1 medium turnip, peeled and quartered
2 small leeks	2 small leeks
1 stalk celery, washed and chopped	1 stalk celery, washed and chopped
8 Dumplings (p. 51)	8 Dumplings (p. 51)

Ask the butcher how long the brisket has been in brine: if longer than 3 days, it may need soaking in cold water for 3 to 4 hours before cooking.

Put the joint in a large pan, cover with cold water and add the bouquet garni. Bring slowly to the boil, then lower the heat to simmer, skim off any scum and simmer gently for 2 hours. Add the onions, carrots, which can be left whole if

small, and turnip to the pan. Clean the leeks (p. 104) and thickly slice the white part. Add the leeks and celery to the pan and continue cooking for 30 minutes.

Make the dumplings and arrange them round the meat. Cover tightly and continue cooking for 15 minutes or until well risen. Place the meat on a warm serving platter and leave it to set before removing the skewers and string. Remove the dumplings and vegetables with a slotted spoon and arrange them round the joint. Garnish with parsley. Discard the bouquet garni and pour 300 ml/½ pint of the stock into a cold saucepan. Remove the fat with kitchen paper (p. 14). Reheat, taste and adjust the seasoning and serve separately in a warm sauce boat.

Poaching Fish

Simmering fish, which is usually called poaching, is a suitable method for cooking whole white fish, fillets and steaks. It is excellent for oily fish such as salmon, salmon trout and trout, and for smoked haddock, cod, whiting and kippered herring.

Smoked Fish

Put the fish in cold water in a sauté pan or skillet, bring to the simmer and cook gently for 10 minutes. Lift out with a fish slice and drain carefully. Serve hot with parsley butter. Smoked cod and whiting are always filleted: finnan haddock and kippers are usually split and left on the bone. You can make a tasty sauce for smoked fillets of haddock, cod and whiting using half fish liquor and half milk. Follow the recipe for Cheese, Lemon or Sour cream sauce on p. 23.

White Fish

Both round and flat fish have a much better flavour if poached in a Fish stock (court bouillon, p. 18). Prepare the fish in the same way as for grilling fish (p. 40), and follow instructions for filleting on p. 150.

Cook the fish either in a sauté pan or skillet on top of the stove, or in a shallow casserole in a slow oven. Bring the fish stock to the boil, lower the heat, and put in the fish in a single layer. The liquid should just cover the fish and no more.

For simple quick dishes, heat sufficient water in the dish to cover the fish, add parsley sprigs, a bay leaf, a piece of onion and/or celery, a few peppercorns, a teaspoon of salt and a dash of lemon juice or vinegar and boil for 5 minutes before adding the fish.

Simmer the fish very gently for 10 to 20 minutes, according to thickness. For large white fish allow 10 minutes per ½ kg/1 lb. The fish is cooked as soon as the flakes of fillets or steaks begin to separate slightly, or the flesh below the head of whole fish starts to shrink from the backbone. Lift it out carefully with a fish slice and keep it warm while you make the sauce. Any sauce will have a greatly improved flavour if you boil the fish stock up briskly without a lid until it is reduced to half before using it.

Any of the White roux sauces, on p. 23, go well with poached fish; replacing half the quantity of milk with cooked fish liquor.

Oily Fish (Salmon, Salmon Trout, Trout)

These can be cooked as for whole white fish, but they have more flavour if wrapped in buttered foil before poaching. If the fish is to be served cold, leave it to cool in the fish liquor. Serve with Hollandaise or Mousseline sauce (p. 29) or Mayonnaise or Tartare sauce (p. 28).

Sole Véronique

METRIC	IMPERIAL
2 sole, skinned and filleted	2 sole, skinned and filleted
juice of 1 lemon	juice of 1 lemon
salt	salt
freshly ground pepper	freshly ground pepper
25 g butter	1 oz butter
225 g green grapes	8 oz green grapes
100 ml dry white wine	4 fl oz dry white wine
2 egg yolks	2 egg yolks
75 ml single cream	3 fl oz single cream

Step 1 Cover the fish bones and skins with cold water. Add the remaining court bouillon ingredients and cook for 20 minutes. Preheat the oven to 190°C, 375°F or gas mark 5. Trim and wash the fillets. Rub them with lemon juice to flavour and whiten and season with salt and pepper. Roll each fillet round your index finger, starting from tail end, with skinned side outward.

Step 4 Beat the egg yolks and cream together in a bowl. Gradually stir in 125 ml/5 fl oz of the reduced liquor.

Court Bouillon
heads, bones and skin of the
fish
cold water to cover
2-3 parsley sprigs
1 bay leaf
1 small onion
6 peppercorns
1 teaspoon salt

Step 2 Spread the bottom of a shallow baking dish with the butter. Arrange the turbans (rolled fish fillets) in the centre of the baking dish, packing them closely together so they will not unroll while cooking. Alternatively, tie each turban with thick thread. Slit and seed the grapes. Fill the centre of each turban with grapes and place the remaining grapes in the dish. Pour in the wine. Strain the court bouillon and add sufficient to come nearly to the top of the turbans, but not to cover them.

Step 3 Lay buttered greaseproof paper over the top of the dish and poach the fish in the oven for about 20 minutes. When cooked, a white curd will appear on the fish. Remove the fish and grapes to a heated serving dish and keep warm. Boil the fish liquor until it is reduced by half and strain it.

Step 5 Place over a saucepan of boiling water, taking care water does not touch the bottom of the bowl. Stir with a wooden spoon until the sauce coats the back of the spoon with a thin cream. Taste and adjust seasoning with lemon juice, salt and pepper. Pour sauce around the fish.

Step 6 For a main course serve with Duchess potatoes (p. 98) and Courgettes (p. 108). For a first course, serve one turban with sauce in an individual ramekin for each person.

If reheating the dish, use a bain-marie (p. 127), as direct heat will curdle the sauce.

Batters Baked Batters

Batter can be used equally well for sweet and savoury dishes. It can be a thin pouring mixture for delicate pancakes or a thick coating texture for fritters, but whatever the consistency, to be successful it must be smooth and lump-free.

Yorkshire Puddings

Brush individual muffin tins with oil or melted fat and heat them on the top shelf of a preheated oven at 220°C, 425°F or gas mark 7. Whisk the basic batter mixture well and pour it into a jug. Half-fill the heated muffin tins and bake in the top of the oven for 20 to 30 minutes or until well risen, crisp and golden. Serve immediately because they toughen as they cool.

Toad in the Hole

Grease a shallow baking dish or roasting pan. Put 8 large beef or pork sausages in the pan and bake in a preheated oven at 220°C, 425°F or gas mark 7, turning occasionally, until they are evenly browned. Arrange the sausages evenly in the dish, whisk the batter well and pour it round the sausages. Return the dish to the oven and bake for 20 to 30 minutes or until the batter is well risen, crisp and golden. Serve immediately with Onion gravy (p. 24) if liked.

Yorkshire Puddings; Toad in the Hole; Cherry Clafoutis; Apple Batter Pudding

Basic Batter Mixture

METRIC	IMPERIAL
100 g plain flour	*4 oz plain flour*
pinch of salt	*pinch of salt*
1 egg	*1 egg*
300 ml milk	*½ pint milk*

Step 1 Sift the flour and salt into a mixing bowl. Make a well in the centre and drop in the egg.

Step 2 Gradually add half the milk to the egg and work the flour into the well, stirring with a wooden spoon so that the flour falls in a thin film onto the liquid.

Step 3 Whisk with a rotary beater until smooth, then gradually whisk in the remaining milk. Leave to stand for 30 minutes to allow the flour to swell.

Apple Batter Pudding

Peel, core and thickly slice ½ kg/1 lb cooking apples. Generously butter a shallow ovenproof dish and heat it in a preheated oven at 220°C, 425°F or gas mark 7. Put in the apples and sprinkle generously with brown sugar. Return the dish to the oven for 10 minutes. Whisk the basic batter mixture and pour it over the apples. Replace the dish in the oven and bake for 30 minutes or until the batter is well risen and golden brown. Dredge with caster sugar and serve immediately.

Cherry Clafoutis

The traditional French Clafoutis, a sweet batter pudding, is made with fat black cherries, but any large ripe cherries will do. You can also use halved stoned plums, apricots or greengages. In winter use drained, canned fruit.

METRIC	IMPERIAL
½ kg ripe cherries	1 lb ripe cherries
50 g plain flour	2 oz plain flour
pinch of salt	pinch of salt
50 g caster sugar	2 oz caster sugar
2 eggs, beaten	2 eggs, beaten
300 ml milk	½ pint milk
40 g butter	1½ oz butter
1 tablespoon cherry brandy or rum (optional)	1 tablespoon cherry brandy or rum (optional)

Remove the stalks and stones from the cherries – a cherry stoner is best for this. Sift the flour and salt into a mixing bowl. Whisk in 2 tablespoons of the caster sugar. Gradually blend in the beaten eggs. Heat the milk until lukewarm and gradually whisk it into the batter.

Melt the butter and brush some of it over a shallow baking dish. Whisk the remaining butter into the batter. Add the cherry brandy or rum, if used. Spread the cherries over the base of the dish and pour the batter over them. Bake in the centre of a preheated oven at 220°C, 425°F or gas mark 7 for 30 to 35 minutes or until golden brown and set. Sprinkle with the remaining sugar and serve hot.

Pancakes

Making Pancakes — Points to Remember

1. You cannot make thin pancakes with thick batter — it should be no thicker than thin cream. 300 ml/½ pint of batter will make about 12 pancakes. Allow two pancakes per serving.
2. Keep a special pan for pancakes and omelettes and wipe it clean with absorbent kitchen paper instead of washing it. To season a new pan or one that has been washed, heat some fat in it, pour it out and wipe the pan before use.
3. The side of the pancake which is cooked first should be the outside when it is rolled or folded.
4. To store pancakes in the refrigerator: do not sugar, leave them flat and pile them on top of each other, with greaseproof paper between each one. To freeze: wrap the pile in foil or cling film and seal carefully. Defrost before reheating in frying pan or oven.

Lemon Pancakes

METRIC	IMPERIAL
300 ml Basic batter mixture (p. 76)	½ pint Basic batter mixture (p. 76)
caster sugar for dredging	caster sugar for dredging
cooking oil or melted lard	cooking oil or melted lard
juice of 1 lemon	juice of 1 lemon

Step 1 Whisk the pancake batter with a rotary beater and pour it into a jug. Place a sheet of greaseproof paper on a working surface beside the stove and dredge the paper with caster sugar. Heat a small thick frying pan about 18-20 cm/7-8 inches in diameter and brush it lightly with cooking oil or fat; too much fat will mix with the batter and make it heavy. When the fat is hot, lift the pan off the burner and pour in just enough batter to cover thinly the base.

Step 2 Twist and tilt the pan so the batter runs evenly over the base. If you have any 'holes', fill them with a little extra batter. If you have too much batter in the pan, pour it off quickly or your pancake will be too thick. Put the pan back on the heat and cook until the batter bubbles all over. Loosen the edges with a palette knife and when the batter is set and bubbly, slip the knife under the pancake and flip it over. If it lands slightly off centre, shake it back into place. Do not poke the pancake or it will tear.

Above: rolling up a
Savoury Stuffed Pancake.
Left: finished dish

Savoury Stuffed Pancakes

METRIC	IMPERIAL
8 thin pancakes	8 thin pancakes
FILLING	FILLING
40 g butter or 40 ml olive oil	1½ oz butter or 1½ fl oz olive oil
1 medium onion, peeled and chopped	1 medium onion, peeled and chopped
100 g mushrooms, washed and sliced	4 oz mushrooms, washed and sliced
2 tablespoons chopped celery	2 tablespoons chopped celery
1 × 440 g can tomatoes	1 × 14 oz can tomatoes
pinch of mixed herbs	pinch of mixed herbs
salt	salt
freshly ground pepper	freshly ground pepper
sugar and lemon juice to taste	sugar and lemon juice to taste
100-175 g frozen prawns or chopped cooked chicken and/or ham	4-6 oz frozen prawns or chopped cooked chicken and/or ham
300 ml Cheese sauce (p. 23)	½ pint Cheese sauce (p. 23)
2 tablespoons grated cheese	2 tablespoons grated cheese
TO GARNISH	TO GARNISH
celery leaves or parsley sprigs	celery leaves or parsley sprigs

Heat the butter or oil and fry the onion, mushrooms and celery until softened. Add the tomatoes and herbs. Season to taste with salt, pepper, sugar and lemon juice. Simmer, uncovered, until reduced to a thick purée. Add the prawns or chopped cooked meat; taste and adjust the seasoning.

Spread the pancakes out flat. Put 2 tablespoons of the filling in the centre of each pancake and fold over the sides to make an envelope. Arrange the filled pancakes, side by side, in a shallow greased gratin dish. Pour hot cheese sauce over the pancakes and sprinkle with grated cheese. The dish may be prepared well in advance up to this stage.

To finish: place the dish in a preheated oven at 200°C, 400°F or gas mark 6 and bake for about 20 minutes or until heated through and bubbly on top. Serve garnished with tufts of celery leaves or parsley sprigs. If using prawn filling, decorate with lemon 'butterflies' as well.

Step 3 When the pancake is golden underneath, flick it out of the pan, upside down, onto the sugared paper. The first side cooked should now be underneath. Sprinkle the top with sugar and then with lemon juice. Pick up the front edge of the paper and tilt it so the pancake rolls up neatly away from you. Lift it with the palette knife on to a warm serving dish. Regrease and reheat the pan for the next pancake.

Note: If making pancakes for savoury dishes omit the sugar and lemon.

Coating Batter

This is thicker than the basic pancake batter as it must cling to the food to be cooked. Sometimes a little oil is added to enrich the batter and increase crispness. The egg can also be separated, with the white being stiffly beaten and folded into the batter just before frying. This gives a lighter batter, which is particularly good for coating shellfish, fruit and vegetables.

Batter is used for coating food which can be cooked quickly, such as fish, shellfish, vegetables, fruit and croquettes made with pre-cooked ingredients. Use deep fat for frying and make sure the fat is the right temperature (p. 66). Use tongs or a 2-pronged cook's fork for dipping the food into the batter. Draw each piece across the edge of the bowl so excess batter drips back into the bowl and not into the deep fat, where it will splutter and burn.

Drain the fried food on absorbent kitchen paper and serve as quickly as possible before it loses its crispness.

Basic Coating Batter

METRIC	IMPERIAL
100 g plain flour	*4 oz plain flour*
pinch of salt	*pinch of salt*
1 egg	*1 egg*
150 ml milk	*¼ pint milk*

Sift the flour and salt into a mixing bowl. Drop the egg into a well in the centre of the flour and blend in the milk as for Basic batter mixture (p. 76). For coating and frying fritters see step-by-step pictures, opposite.

Light Continental Batter

This thin crispy batter is excellent for frying prawns, scampi, scallops, cauliflower sprigs, onion rings, mushroom caps, sliced cucumber, courgettes and aubergines. The last three should have their moisture extracted, see Sauté vegetables (p. 71). Shellfish and onion rings should be well dried and tossed in flour before being dipped in the batter.

METRIC	IMPERIAL
100 g plain flour	*4 oz plain flour*
pinch of salt	*pinch of salt*
1 tablespoon vegetable oil	*1 tablespoon vegetable oil*
300 ml tepid water	*½ pint tepid water*
1 egg white	*1 egg white.*

Sift flour and salt into a mixing bowl. Add the oil to the tepid water and blend it gradually into the flour as for Basic pancake batter (p. 76). Just before using, whip the egg white until stiff but not brittle. Whisk the batter and fold in the egg white evenly.

Fruit Fritters

METRIC	IMPERIAL
300 ml Basic coating batter, without egg	½ pint Basic coating batter, without egg
2 bananas	2 bananas
2 apples, cooking or dessert	2 apples, cooking or dessert
juice of 1 lemon	juice of 1 lemon
4 pineapple slices, fresh or canned	4 pineapple sliced, fresh or canned
4 apricots or plums	4 apricots or plums
1 egg white	1 egg white
1-2 teaspoons cinnamon	1-2 teaspoons cinnamon
caster sugar	caster sugar

Step 1 Peel the bananas and cut into quarters. Peel the apples, cut into thick rings and core with a corer. Sprinkle the bananas and apples with lemon juice to prevent them browning. Cut a fresh, peeled pineapple into slices and remove the core. Drain the canned pineapple slices and dry on absorbent kitchen paper. Halve and stone the apricots or plums.

Step 2 Prepare the deep fat (p. 66). Put in the frying basket and heat the fat to 190°C, 375°F. Just before frying the fritters, whisk the egg white until stiff but not brittle and, with a concave spatula (p. 36) or large cook's spoon, fold it into the batter quickly and evenly.

Step 3 Dip the prepared fruit into the batter, using a 2-pronged cook's fork. The prongs can be inserted into the hole in the centre of the apple and pineapple rings. Draw the cooked fruit across the edge of the bowl so excess batter drops back into it. Lower the fruit into the fat and fry until the batter is crisp and golden. Do not overcrowd the pan. Use a slotted spoon to turn the fritters.

Step 4 Lift the frying basket out of the pan and allow the fat to drain back into the pan. Place the fritters on absorbent kitchen paper to drain. Mix the cinnamon with 2 to 3 tablespoons caster sugar and sprinkle it over the fritters. Keep the fritters warm while reheating the oil and frying the next batch. Serve immediately, arranged on a paper doily in a warm serving dish and hand extra caster sugar separately.

Cauliflower florets, onion rings, prawns, cucumber slices and mushrooms coated in Light Continental Batter and deep-fried

Pastries Shortcrust Pastry

All pastry doughs, with the exception of choux (for éclairs) and hot water crust (for raised pies), need to be kept cool during making — use cold equipment and ingredients and keep fingers cool for mixing. On the other hand, a hot oven is essential for successful baking.

It is best to use plain flour. A variety of fats are suitable — sometimes singly, sometimes mixed — e.g. butter, margarine, lard, solid vegetable fats, proprietary blended fats and, for a few special pastries, vegetable oil. The proportion of fat to flour determines the richness of the pastry. For plain short doughs, the fat is rubbed in and for rich flaky doughs it is rolled in.

The amount of water needed varies according to the type of flour used. Too little water makes the dough crumbly and difficult to roll out and shape, and too much produces a hard pastry. You need just enough to make the dough soft but not sticky. If you add too much water and have to use more flour to make it manageable, it will alter the proportion of flour to fat and give you a pastry less rich than desired. For the same reason, do not work in too much flour while rolling out the pastry.

Never stretch the pastry when putting it over a pie or lining a tin as it will shrink back during baking and distort the shape of the pie or flan.

When a recipe says 225 g/8 oz of pastry, this means pastry dough made with 225 g/8 oz flour excluding fat.

Plain Shortcrust

This is a basic pastry in which the fat is rubbed into the flour and produces a crisp, biscuit-like texture.

METRIC	IMPERIAL
225 g plain flour	*8 oz plain flour*
pinch of salt	*pinch of salt*
100 g margarine or lard (or half and half)	*4 oz margarine or lard (or half and half)*
cold water to mix	*cold water to mix*

Makes 225 g/8 oz pastry

Step 1 Sift the flour and salt into a mixing bowl. Cut up the fat into chunks, toss it into the flour and rub it in with the tips of the fingers. Lift your hands well above the bowl to incorporate as much air as possible.

Step 2 When the mixture is the consistency of breadcrumbs, shake the bowl so that any lumps rise to the surface and rub them in. Do not over-do the rubbing or the dough will become sticky before the water is added.

Lining a Flan Ring

Step 1 Place an ungreased flan ring, fluted or plain, on a greased baking sheet. Roll out the pastry into a circle, about 5 mm/¼ inch thick, which will extend about 3.5 cm/1½ inches beyond the flan ring all round.

Step 2 Raise the pastry circle slightly above the board, with both hands, and let it fall gently back so it can shrink now, and not during baking. Fold the pastry into a five-sided shape small enough to fit inside the flan ring.

Step 3 Lift folded pastry into the flan ring. Open it out and carefully ease it into the angle all round the base with the right forefinger. Do not stretch the pastry.

Step 4 Press the pastry into the flutes with a floured forefinger, holding the ring steady with the other hand.

Step 3 Mix in the cold water, a little at a time, using a knife with a rounded blade edge. When the dough is beginning to bind, use the fingers of one hand to gather the mixture together. Add more water if it is too dry and crumbly.

Step 4 Work the dough into a soft ball, leaving the bowl clean and dry. The dough can be used right away or put in a cool place until required. If refrigerating or freezing, wrap the pastry in foil or polythene to prevent it drying out.

Step 5 Lightly flour the pastry board and rolling pin. Knead the dough lightly and shape it into a round for a round dish, or oval for an oval dish.

Step 6 Roll out with short jerky rolls away from yourself. A 'steamroller' action will roll out the air bubbles. Move the pastry about on the board to make sure it does not stick, but never turn it upside down.

Baking Blind

Flan cases are often baked blind (empty) when they are to be filled with uncooked or cold filling.

Step 5 Roll the rolling pin across the top of the ring to cut off the surplus pastry. Remove the trimmings.

Step 1 Preheat the oven to 200°C, 400°F or gas mark 6. Prick the base of the flan all over with a fork. Line it with a piece of greaseproof paper and cover with a layer of dried beans to keep the pastry from rising during baking.

Step 2 Bake the flan in the oven for 15 to 20 minutes or until the sides of the flan are crisp and set. Lift out the paper and beans and lift off the ring, using an oven glove or thick cloth.

Step 3 Return the pastry to the oven for 5 minutes to crisp the base.

Rich Shortcrust

METRIC	IMPERIAL
100 g plain flour	*4 oz plain flour*
pinch of salt	*pinch of salt*
75 g butter and lard, or	*3 oz butter and lard, or*
margarine and lard	*margarine and lard*
1 egg yolk	*1 egg yolk*
1-2 tablespoons water	*1-2 tablespoons water*
Makes 100 g/4 oz pastry	

Sift the flour and salt into a mixing bowl. Cut up the fat and rub it in as for Plain shortcrust (p. 82). Beat the egg yolk and water together and stir it into the flour, adding more water if required. Work to a soft, but not sticky dough. Knead the dough lightly on a floured board and leave it to relax in a cool place for at least 30 minutes before rolling it out. Bake in a preheated oven at 200°C, 400°F or gas mark 6.
  Makes one 15-18 cm/6-7 inch flan case.

Sweet Shortcrust

METRIC	IMPERIAL
175 g plain flour	*6 oz plain flour*
pinch of salt	*pinch of salt*
100 g butter or margarine	*4 oz butter or margarine*
25 g caster sugar	*1 oz caster sugar*
cold water to mix	*cold water to mix*
1 egg yolk	*1 egg yolk*
Makes 175 g/6 oz pastry	

Sift the flour and salt into a mixing bowl. Cut up the fat and rub in as for Plain shortcrust (p. 82). Mix in the sugar. Add 2 tablespoons cold water to beaten egg yolk and proceed as for Rich shortcrust (above). Leave to relax for 30 minutes before using. Bake in a preheated oven at 200°C, 400°F or gas mark 6.
  Makes one 18-20 cm/7-8 inch flan or about 18 tartlet cases or barquettes (boat shapes).

Cheese Shortcrust

METRIC	IMPERIAL
175 g plain flour	*6 oz plain flour*
¼ teaspoon salt	*¼ teaspoon salt*
pinch of dried mustard	*pinch of dried mustard*
75 g butter and lard, or	*3 oz butter and lard, or*
margarine and lard	*margarine and lard*
75 g mature dry Cheddar	*3 oz mature dry Cheddar*
cheese, grated	*cheese, grated*
1 egg yolk	*1 egg yolk*
cold water to mix	*cold water to mix*
Makes 150 g/6 oz pastry	

Sift the flour, salt and mustard into a mixing bowl. Cut up the fat and rub in as for Plain shortcrust (p. 82). Mix in the grated cheese thoroughly. Mix the egg yolk with 2 tablespoons cold water and stir it in, adding extra water as needed. Bind the ingredients into a soft but not sticky dough. Knead the dough on a floured board. Leave the pastry to relax in a cool place before rolling it out. Bake in a preheated oven at 200°C, 400°F or gas mark 6.
  Makes one 18-20 cm/7-8 inch flan case or 18 tartlet cases or barquettes (boat shapes).

Cheese Straws

Roll the Cheese shortcrust pastry out into a strip 10 cm/4 inches wide. Trim the edges. Using an 8 cm/3½ inch scone cutter, cut some rounds from the pastry. With a 6 cm/2½ inch scone cutter, cut rounds from the centre of the large circles and place both on a greased baking tray. With a sharp knife, cut strips off the rectangle, place on a baking tray. Bake in a preheated oven at 220°C, 425°F or gas mark 7 for 5 to 7 minutes. Cool on a wire tray. Arrange in bundles with straws pushed through circles. Sandwich the little rounds together with anchovy paste.

Anchovy Plaits and Twists

Cut strips of Cheese shortcrust pastry as for Cheese straws (above). Lay two pastry strips side by side. Put an anchovy fillet in the middle and plait the anchovy fillet with the pastry strips. Damp the ends of the pastry and seal together. Alternatively, twist one pastry strip with an anchovy fillet, damp and seal the ends. Bake plaits and twists in a preheated oven at 220°C, 425°F or gas mark 7 for 5 to 7 minutes. Serve hot or cold.

Quiche Lorraine

METRIC
1 × 18 cm cooked flan case,
  made with Plain or Cheese
  shortcrust
FILLING
15 g butter or margarine
1 tablespoon chopped onion
2 rashers streaky bacon,
  chopped
225 ml single cream or
  evaporated milk
50 g Cheddar cheese, grated
1 egg, beaten
salt
freshly ground pepper
paprika pepper

IMPERIAL
1 × 7 inch cooked flan case,
  made with Plain or Cheese
  shortcrust
FILLING
½ oz butter or margarine
1 tablespoon chopped onion
2 rashers streaky bacon,
  chopped
8 fl oz single cream or
  evaporated milk
2 oz Cheddar cheese, grated
1 egg, beaten
salt
freshly ground pepper
paprika pepper

Heat the butter and fry the onion and bacon until they begin to change colour. Add the cream or evaporated milk and heat until it has a rim of bubbles, but do not boil. Remove the pan from the heat and mix in the grated cheese. Stir until the cheese has melted then mix in the beaten egg. Season to taste with salt, pepper and paprika. Pour the mixture into the flan case and bake in a preheated oven at 180°C, 350°F or gas mark 4 for 20 minutes or until the filling is set and golden. Serve hot garnished with grilled bacon rolls or cold with tossed green salad, which is excellent for picnics.

Variations

Mushroom Quiche
Follow the recipe for Quiche Lorraine, but fry 100 g/4 oz sliced mushrooms with the bacon and onion. Serve hot, topped with fried mushroom caps, turned black side up and garnished with paprika.

Asparagus Quiche
Follow the recipe for Quiche Lorraine, using cream. Cover the base of the flan case with cooked asparagus tips, fresh or canned, and pour over the heated filling. Bake as for Quiche Lorraine and serve hot garnished with asparagus tips or watercress sprigs. This makes a delightful first course.

Asparagus Barquettes
Bake pastry shells in boat shapes. Put 2 asparagus tips in each one and pour over the filling. Bake for 15 minutes or until set, in a preheated oven at 180°C, 350°F or gas mark 4. Serve hot or cold as a buffet snack.

Cheese Straws; Anchovy Plaits and Twists; Asparagus Barquettes; Asparagus Quiche; Quiche Lorraine

Suet Crust Pastry

This is made by the same method as Plain shortcrust with the same proportion of fat to flour, i.e. twice as much flour as fat. Suet is the fat which surrounds ox kidney. You can prepare your own by cutting off the surplus fat from a beef sirloin and grating it finely – dip the lump of suet frequently in flour to prevent it sticking to the grater. Prepared shredded suet is readily available in small packs. Store it in the refrigerator or a cool, dry place, to stop it getting sticky. It can be baked or steamed and should always be served hot.

Right: Baked Roly Poly; Steamed Roly Poly Pudding

Suet Crust Pastry

METRIC	IMPERIAL
225 g plain flour and 3 teaspoons baking powder	*8 oz plain flour and 3 teaspoons baking powder*
or 225 g self-raising flour	*or 8 oz self-raising flour*
pinch of salt	*pinch of salt*
100 g shredded suet	*4 oz shredded suet*
cold water to mix	*cold water to mix*
Makes 225 g/8 oz pastry	

Sift the flour, baking powder and salt into a mixing bowl. Add the suet and toss lightly in the flour until well mixed. Stir in sufficient cold water to bind the ingredients into a soft but not sticky dough.

Baked Roly Poly

Make as for Steamed roly poly pudding and turn, seam side down, onto a piece of greased foil just large enough to come halfway up the roll. Tie loosely with 2 pieces of string. Cut 4 slits in the top of the roll to allow the steam to escape. Brush with milk and sprinkle with sugar. Bake in a preheated oven at 200°C, 400°F or gas mark 6 for 30 minutes or until well risen and golden. Serve hot with cream or Custard (p. 30).

Steamed Roly Poly Pudding

 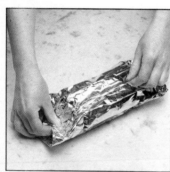

To prepare the pastry for steaming, roll up and seal in greased foil.

Roll out 225 g/8 oz Suet crust pastry into a rectangle about 25 × 20 cm/10 × 8 inches and 5 mm/¼ inch thick. Spread it evenly with warm jam or mincemeat, leaving a 1 cm/½ inch border all round. Fold this border over the filling and brush with water. Roll up, fairly loosely, from the shortest side. Press the top edge firmly down and seal the ends of the roll by pressing the pastry edges together. Turn the roll seam side down, on to a sheet of greased foil, which is large enough to wrap round the roll and leave space for the pastry to swell. Seal the foil at each end by pressing the edges firmly together. Place the roll in the steamer (p. 128) and cook for 1½ to 2 hours. When cooked, open the foil and roll the pudding carefully onto a warm serving plate and dust with caster sugar. Serve with Custard (p. 30) or Fruit sauce (p. 31).

Steak and Kidney Pudding

METRIC	IMPERIAL
½ kg stewing steak	*1¼ lb stewing steak*
225 g ox kidney	*8 oz ox kidney*
flour for coating	*flour for coating*
225 g Suet crust pastry	*8 oz Suet crust pastry*
salt	*salt*
freshly ground pepper	*freshly ground pepper*
approx. 125 ml beef stock or water	*approx. ¼ pint beef stock or water*

Step 1 Grease a 1.2 litre/2 pint pudding basin. Cut the steak into 3 cm/1¼ inch chunks, discarding any fat and gristle. Cut the kidney into smaller pieces, discarding the fatty core. Toss the meat in flour, in a paper bag, until it is well coated.

Step 2 Roll out the suet crust into a circle 5 mm/¼ inch thick and 10 cm/4 inches all round larger than the top of the basin. Cut a quarter out of the circle and reserve for the lid. It will also make the lining pastry fit better.

Step 3 Lift the pastry into the basin, centre it carefully and ease it into the basin so the cut edges overlap slightly. Damp and seal these edges. Press the pastry evenly against side of basin so there are no pleats.

Step 4 Trim excess pastry off around the top edge of the basin. Put in the steak and kidney, seasoning each layer with salt and pepper. Add sufficient stock or water to come a quarter of the way up the filling. Fold pastry edge over on top of filling, brush with water.

Step 5 Gather the remaining triangle of pastry into a ball, and roll it out into a circle to fit the top of the basin. Lay it on top of the filling and press the pastry edges together. Cover and steam (p. 128) for 3½ to 4 hours.

Step 6 Remove the pudding from the steamer and allow it to shrink slightly before turning it out (p. 129). Alternatively, wrap the basin in a clean napkin and serve the pudding in the basin. Serve with Onion gravy (p. 24) if wished.

Rough Puff Pastry

This is the simplest of the rich, flaky-textured pastries. Rich pastries are flaky-textured because they contain a high proportion of fat to flour. The fat is rolled into the dough instead of being rubbed in as for shortcrust. This pastry is light and crisp when hot, but becomes heavy when cold. It is excellent for hot meat and game pie, fruit tarts and sausage rolls. It freezes and reheats very well.

METRIC	IMPERIAL
225 g plain flour	*8 oz plain flour*
pinch of salt	*pinch of salt*
175 g butter and lard or	*6 oz butter and lard or*
* margarine and lard*	* margarine and lard*
1 teaspoon lemon juice	*1 teaspoon lemon juice*
cold water to mix	*cold water to mix*
Makes 225 g/8 oz pastry	

Step 1 Sift the flour and salt into a mixing bowl. Cut the fat into cubes about 1½ cm/¾ inch. Add the fat to the flour and toss it lightly until it is well covered with flour.

Step 4 With a floured rolling pin and using short jerky rolls, roll out the dough into a rectangle about 1 cm/½ inch thick. Keep the edges and corners neat. Mark the pastry across into 3 equal parts.

Sausage Rolls

METRIC	IMPERIAL
225 g Rough puff pastry	*8 oz Rough puff pastry*
½ kg sausage meat	*1 lb sausage meat*
1 beaten egg, for glazing	*1 beaten egg, for glazing*

Step 1 Preheat the oven to 200°C, 425°F or gas mark 7. Roll out the pastry into a rectangle 5 mm/¼ inch thick and about 15 cm/6 inches wide, divide it lengthwise in half. Divide the sausage meat in half and, on a floured board, roll it into 2 long thin sausage shapes. Place one on each pastry strip, just right of the centre. Brush the pastry edges with beaten egg and fold the pastry over the sausage meat.

Step 2 Add the lemon juice to the water and stir it into the flour without breaking up the lumps of fat and using just sufficient to bind the ingredients into dough.

Step 3 With floured fingers, gather the dough into a ball and put it on a floured board. Shape it into a rectangular brick using hands and a rolling pin.

Step 5 Fold up the bottom third, keeping fingers inside and the thumbs on top of the pastry, and seal the edges so you have a little 'tent' full of air. Fold the top third of pastry down and seal in the same way.

Step 6 Seal the edges with the rolling pin. Give the pastry a quarter turn to the left or right.
  Repeat the rolling, folding in air and turning, 3 to 4 times, until no streaks of fat are visible in the dough. Keep the rolling pin floured and clear of fat or it will stick to the pastry. Chill the pastry until it is cold and stiff before using.

Step 2 Press the pastry edges firmly together and knock up with the back of the knife like a pie edging (p. 91). Cut the pastry rolls into equal 5 cm/2 inch lengths or larger if preferred. Place on a dampened baking tray and brush with beaten egg. Cut 2 or 3 slits across the top of each roll for the steam to escape.

Step 3 Bake just above the centre of the oven for 25 to 30 minutes or until well risen and golden brown. Serve hot with mustard.
  If serving the rolls cold, use Flaky pastry (p. 92) instead of rough puff pastry.

Steak, Kidney and Mushroom Pie

METRIC	IMPERIAL
Steak and kidney pie filling (p. 55)	*Steak and kidney pie filling (p. 55)*
100 g mushrooms, sliced	*4 oz mushrooms, sliced*
225 g Rough puff pastry	*8 oz Rough puff pastry*
1 beaten egg, for glazing	*1 beaten egg, for glazing*
parsley sprig for garnish	*parsley sprig for garnish*

Put a pie funnel in the centre of a 1.2 litre/2 pint pie dish. This is to make a vent for steam to escape during baking, so the pastry will not be soggy underneath. Pack the cold filling round the funnel and cover with the sliced mushrooms.

Covering Pie with Pastry

Step 1 Roll out the pastry 5 mm/¼ inch thick and cut a strip of pastry, the same width as the lip of the pie dish, off the outside edge of the pastry. Damp the lip with a brush and press the pastry strip firmly on. Damp and press the joins together.

Step 2 Damp the pastry strip. Roll the rest of the pastry on to the rolling pin and unroll it over the dish.

Step 3 Press the pastry edges together on the lip of the dish. Trim edges around rim with a sharp knife.

Step 4 With the back of the forefinger of the left hand, press the pastry lid down and slightly off the edge of the pie dish, and with the back of the knife, held horizontally in the other hand, knock the pastry back, flaking the edge.

Step 5 Flute the edge by pressing down with the left thumb, and pulling the pastry back towards the pie dish with the back of the knife held vertically in the other hand. Pull the pastry with the knife do not cut it.

Step 6 Insert a skewer into the pie funnel, through the pastry, to make a hole for the steam to escape. Cut a slit on top of the pie on each side of the funnel. Brush the top of the pie with beaten egg, but not the flaked edge.

Decorating Top of Pie

Step 1 Roll out the pastry trimmings and cut a strip 2.5 cm/1 inch wide and cut diagonally across to make 6 diamond shapes for leaves. With the back of the knife, mark 'veins' down the centre of each leaf and short lines on either side.

Step 2 Brush the top surface of each leaf with beaten egg. Hold the points of the leaf at each end and twist. Place the leaf in position on top of the pie – take care not to block the slits for steam.

Step 3 Roll out another strip of pastry 3½ cm/1½ inches wide. Cut evenly spaced slits three quarters of the way across to form a fringe. Brush with beaten egg. Roll the pastry strip round a skewer with the point protruding 2.5 cm/1 inch beyond the uncut edge.

Step 4 Insert the point of the skewer into the pie funnel. Press the base of the roll of pastry firmly onto the pie. Remove the skewer and with the point open out the petals of the pastry flower.

Baking the Pie

Preheat the oven to 220°C, 425°F or gas mark 7. Place the pie on a baking sheet and bake on the upper shelf for 20 minutes or until the pastry is well risen and turning brown. Then reduce the heat to 200°C, 400°F or gas mark 6 for a further 30 minutes for the pie to cook through. If the pastry is turning too brown, cover the top with a paper bag to protect it. Serve the pie hot, garnished with a sprig of parsley.

Flaky Pastry

This is not quite as rich as puff pastry but when properly made it is very light and flaky. Flaky pastry can be eaten either hot or cold and is excellent for vol-au-vent cases, jam puffs, etc. Do not grease baking trays for rich pastry, but damp them lightly.

Flaky Pastry

Makes 225 g/8 oz pastry

METRIC
225 g plain flour
pinch of salt
75 g butter
75 g lard
1 teaspoon lemon juice
1 cup cold water

IMPERIAL
8 oz plain flour
pinch of salt
3 oz butter
3 oz lard
1 teaspoon lemon juice
1 cup cold water

When the pastry is made (step 6) put it in a polythene bag and chill it in the refrigerator for at least 30 minutes until it is cool and firm. If the dough becomes sticky during making, chill pastry between rolls until stiffened. Keep the board and rolling pin clean and dry and well floured to prevent sticking.

Step 1 Sift the flour and salt into a mixing bowl. Blend the butter and lard into a round then divide it into four. Rub one quarter of the fat into the flour as for Shortcrust (p. 82). Add the lemon juice to the water and add sufficient to bind the fat and flour into a soft but not sticky dough.

Step 2 Gather the dough into a ball and knead it lightly on a floured board. With a floured rolling pin, roll out the dough with short jerky strokes into a rectangle about 38 × 18 cm/15 × 7 inches. Keep the edges and corners neat.

Step 3 Mark the rectangle across into three equal parts. With a rounded knife, flake the second quarter of fat evenly over the top two-thirds of pastry, leaving a 1 cm/½ inch border.

Step 4 With floured fingers, keeping thumbs on top and fingers underneath, fold over the bottom third of pastry and seal the edges firmly to incorporate air.

Step 5 Fold the top third of pastry down and seal in air in the same way. Seal the edges with the rolling pin and give the dough a quarter turn to the left or right.

Step 6 Flour the board and rolling pin and roll out again into a rectangle. Mark into three and flake the third quantity of fat onto the top two-thirds of the rectangle. Fold, seal and give a quarter turn as in Step 5. Roll again and repeat Step 6 with last quantity of fat. Repeat step 6 without adding any fat.

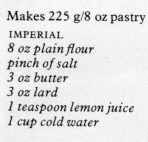

Prawn Vol-Au-Vent

METRIC	IMPERIAL
225 g Flaky pastry	*8 oz Flaky pastry*
1 egg, beaten	*1 egg, beaten*
Prawn filling (see below)	*Prawn filling (see below)*
TO GARNISH	TO GARNISH
lemon	*lemon*
watercress sprigs	*watercress sprigs*

Filling for Vol-Au-Vent

METRIC	IMPERIAL
50 g button mushrooms,	*2 oz button mushrooms,*
sliced	*sliced*
100 g peeled prawns	*4 oz peeled prawns*
40 g butter	*40 g butter*
300 ml Parsley coating sauce	*½ pint Parsley coating sauce*
(p. 23)	*(p. 23)*
lemon juice to taste	*lemon juice to taste*

Fry the mushrooms and prawns lightly in butter and add them to the hot parsley sauce. Sharpen to taste with lemon juice.

Step 1 Preheat the oven to 230°C, 450°F or gas mark 8. Roll out chilled flaky pastry 5 mm/¼ inch thick. With a floured 7.5 cm/3 inch pastry cutter, cut out rounds and place half on a damp baking tray. With a 4.5 cm/1¾ inch cutter, cut the centre out of the remaining rounds, leaving rings. Place trimmings in a pile on each other (do not knead). Reroll and cut as before.

Step 2 Prick the large round with a fork and damp the edges lightly. Place a pastry ring on each one and press down. Mark a criss-cross pattern with a knife on top of the rings and brush with beaten egg. Glaze the remaining little rounds with egg and place on a separate tray as they will cook very quickly. They will serve as lids.

Step 3 Bake the pastry on the upper shelf of the oven for 10 minutes until well risen and set. Remove the tray of lids. Lower the heat to 220°C, 425°F or gas mark 7 and cook the cases for a further 10 minutes or until crisp and golden brown. Remove the soft dough from inside cases and from the bottom of the lids. Cool on a wire rack.

To serve, heat the cases in a preheated oven at 190°C, 375°F or gas mark 5 for about 15 minutes. Place on a warm serving dish. Fill each with hot Prawn filling and put on the lids. Garnish with quarter slices of lemon and watercress sprigs.

Choux Pastry

This French pastry is first cooked in a saucepan and then baked in a hot oven to make éclairs and cream buns, etc.

Choux Pastry

METRIC	IMPERIAL
75 g plain flour	*3 oz plain flour*
25 g butter or margarine	*1 oz butter or margarine*
150 ml water	*¼ pint water*
2 eggs, beaten	*2 eggs, beaten*
Makes 75 g/3 oz pastry	

Step 1 Sift the flour onto a piece of greaseproof paper. Melt the fat in the water in a small saucepan over gentle heat. Do not allow the water to boil before the fat has melted as it will evaporate and reduce the quantity. Bring the water to the boil, remove pan from heat and tip in the flour all at once.

Step 2 Beat with a wooden spoon until the dough is smooth. Return the pan to moderate heat and continue beating until the dough forms a ball and leaves the sides of the pan clean. Do not overheat or the dough will become oily.

Step 3 Cool the dough slightly and start adding the beaten eggs, a spoonful at a time. Beat thoroughly between each addition. If the egg is added too quickly, the dough will become too slack and it will not be possible to pipe it.

Eclairs

These can be made 7.5-10 cm/3-4 inches long and filled either with whipped cream or flavoured custard and coated with Coffee or Lemon glacé icing (p. 142), or Chocolate glacé icing (opposite). They should be made on the day they are required as the baked pastry becomes tough.

Strawberry or Raspberry Éclairs

Fill éclairs with whipped cream and sliced strawberries or whole raspberries and coat with Lemon glacé icing, tinted with pink colouring.

Chocolate Eclairs; Coffee Eclairs; Raspberry Eclairs

Vegetables

Vegetables are essential to a healthy diet as they provide vitamins, mineral salts, roughage, and in the case of pulses, protein.

They also add variety and colour to meals, when served either as side or main dishes. Vegetables are usually grouped under the headings of tubers (potatoes), root vegetables, leaves, stems, pods, gourds, bulbs and pulses.

Strictly speaking rhubarb is a stem vegetable, but is cooked and served as fruit, while tomatoes are fruit which are eaten raw or cooked as a vegetable.

Potatoes

New Potatoes

The first home-grown new potatoes come into season from the end of May and are available until the end of July; then the next early varieties start and go on until mid-September. Buy new potatoes fresh in small quantities because they quickly lose their unique earthy flavour. They should not be kept more than two or three days.

New potatoes are best boiled and served hot, or cold as salad. They can also be roasted and chipped, but are too waxy to mash or bake in their skins. Look for new potatoes which are dry and have tender skins which rub off easily between thumb and finger. Many people prefer to cook and serve the first small new potatoes in their skins or peel them after cooking. This conserves the vitamin C as well as flavour. For the same reason, new potatoes should be dropped into salted water which is already boiling.

To boil: Put sufficient water in a saucepan so the potatoes will just be covered. Add salt (1 teaspoon salt to ½ kg/1 pound potatoes) and a sprig of fresh mint and bring to the boil.

Scrub the potatoes or scrape them if preferred, and cook gently in boiling water for 20 minutes or until tender, according to size. Strain the potatoes through a colander, place them over an empty hot saucepan and cover with crumpled clean cloth to keep them warm and dry. Peel if desired.

Put 50 g/2 oz butter per ½ kg/1 pound potatoes in a warm saucepan and, when melted, add the potatoes and shake over gentle heat until well coated. Serve in a hot dish and sprinkle generously with chopped fresh mint or parsley.

Drying off boiled potatoes

Coating potatoes in melted butter

Pommes Maître D'Hôtel

METRIC	IMPERIAL
½ kg new potatoes	1 lb new potatoes
50 g butter	2 oz butter
1 shallot, peeled and chopped	1 shallot, peeled and chopped
2 tablespoons chopped parsley	2 tablespoons chopped parsley
salt	salt
freshly ground pepper	freshly ground pepper
150 ml milk or single cream	¼ pint milk or single cream

Scrub the potatoes and boil them in their skins. Peel and slice fairly thinly. Melt the butter in a flameproof dish. Layer the potatoes with the shallot and parsley and season each layer with salt and pepper. Bring the milk or cream nearly to the boil and pour it over the potatoes. Heat gently until hot through, but do not boil.

Maincrop (Old Potatoes)

Maincrop potatoes are available from early October and can be safely bought in larger quantities, provided they are stored in the dark, away from strong sunlight or fluorescent lighting, to avoid greening. The temperature should be cool or they will sprout and shrivel, but not too cold or they may develop a sweet flavour.

There are many maincrop varieties. King Edward and Red King are very good all round cookers for general purposes. Kerrs Pink, with their mealy texture, are very suitable for boiling and mashing and for potato cakes and scones. Majestic keep well and are excellent for chips, but not so good for all purposes because they tend to discolour.

To boil: Choose potatoes of the same size, peel and cut into pieces of similar size, so they will cook evenly. Cover with cold, well salted water, allow 1 teaspoon for ½ kg/1 pound potatoes. Put on a lid and bring to the boil. Remove the lid, lower the heat and simmer steadily until tender. Drain in a colander and dry as for new potatoes (see facing page) or put in a warm dish in a low oven until required. This helps to give them a floury texture. Serve garnished with chopped fresh parsley.

To roast: Select medium potatoes of even size and peel, or cut larger potatoes to even size. Bring to simmer as for boiled potatoes, but cook for only 10 minutes, drain and dry well.

Heat dripping or lard in a roasting pan in a preheated oven at 200-220°C, 400-425°F or gas mark 6-7 until hazing. Put in potatoes and turn in the hot fat. Place in top of the oven and roast for about 40 minutes, turning once. Alternatively, roast in the dripping round the joint for the last 50 to 60 minutes. Remove with slotted spoon, drain on absorbent kitchen paper and serve as soon as possible. If keeping warm in a low oven, do not cover or they will lose their crispness.

Pommes Maître D'Hôtel;
Roast Potatoes

Mashed Potatoes

METRIC	IMPERIAL
½ kg old potatoes	1 lb old potatoes
25-50 g butter or margarine	1-2 oz butter or margarine
2 tablespoons hot milk	2 tablespoons hot milk
salt	salt
freshly ground pepper	freshly ground pepper
pinch of nutmeg (optional)	pinch of nutmeg (optional)

Step 1 Peel the potatoes thinly and cut into chunks of even size. Cover with salted water, bring to the boil and simmer gently for 10 to 20 minutes according to size. Do not over-cook or the mash will be watery. Drain well, dry off in pan over low heat. Mash thoroughly with potato masher or put through a mouli.

Step 2 Replace the pan over low heat and beat in the butter and hot milk with a kichamajig or wooden spoon until fluffy. Season well with salt, freshly ground pepper and a pinch of nutmeg, if liked.

Duchess Potatoes

Piping potato mixture into pyramids

Finished potatoes, glazed and browned

Boil and sieve the potatoes as above and beat in 25 g/1 oz butter, 1 egg yolk and sufficient hot milk to give a creamy consistency. Put into a forcing bag with a large rose nozzle and pipe onto a greased baking tray into pyramids, rings or nests. Bake in a preheated oven at 220°C, 425°F or gas mark 7 for 20 minutes or until golden. For a shiny glazed finish, remove from the oven when set, brush with beaten egg yolk and return to oven to brown.

Baked Potatoes

Select large or medium potatoes, scrub well and prick all over with a cook's fork. This is to allow the steam to escape during cooking, otherwise the potatoes may burst in the oven. For a crisp skin, brush with oil. Place on a baking sheet and bake in a preheated oven at 200-220°C, 400-425°F or gas mark 6-7 for 1 hour or until soft.

When cooked, cut two slits crosswise in the top and gently squeeze the bottom of the potato until the cross opens. Push in a good pat of butter, top with a parsley sprig and serve piping hot with salt and pepper.

Alternatively, when cooked, cut an oval piece from the top of each potato, or if a large potato, cut in half lengthwise. Scoop out the pulp into a basin, beat with butter and seasoning and put back into shell. Ruffle the top with a fork and reheat in oven or brown under grill.

Baked Stuffed Potatoes

Mix potato pulp with cream or soured cream and chives; grated Cheddar cheese and paprika pepper; chopped cooked mushrooms and parsley; chopped cooked meat, chicken or ham, or crisp fried and diced bacon.

Baked Potatoes and Baked Stuffed Potatoes

Root Vegetables

Carrots, Parsnips, Turnips, Swedes

To prepare root vegetables for cooking, scrub them and scrape off thin skins or peel tough, thick ones. Rinse in clean water, slice if mature, leave whole or quarter if young and tender. Allow ½ kg/1 lb for 3 to 4 servings.

To boil: Barely cover the prepared vegetables with boiling water, adding 1 teaspoon salt to each ½ kg/1 lb vegetables. Cover and simmer gently for 20 minutes or until tender when tested with a skewer. Drain and keep the water to make sauce, gravy or soup. Toss the vegetables in melted butter and fresh herbs, or coat with a sauce.

To casserole: This method conserves the flavour and nutritive value of the vegetables better than boiling. For each ½ kg/1 lb vegetables, melt 15 g/½ oz butter or margarine in a flameproof casserole. Add vegetables, cover closely and sweat for 5 to 10 minutes on low heat. Add 150 ml/¼ pint water with 1 teaspoon salt, cover and cook very gently for 20 to 30 minutes on top of the stove or 30 to 40 minutes in a preheated oven at 150°C, 300°F or gas mark 2. Sprinkle with chopped parsley and serve with the liquid.

Skirlie-Mirlie; Glazed Carrots; Buttered Turnips with Mustard; Roast Parsnips

Turnips

Early turnips are available from April to July. While they are young they are often sold in bunches. Trim, peel, wash, quarter and boil or casserole. Maincrop turnips are in season from August to March and, although coarser, are good for flavouring soups and sauces.

Buttered Turnips with Mustard

METRIC	IMPERIAL
½ kg young white turnips, peeled	1 lb young white turnips, peeled
50 g unsalted butter	2 oz unsalted butter
1 teaspoon salt	1 teaspoon salt
1-2 tablespoons French mustard	1-2 tablespoons French mustard
1-2 tablespoons chopped fresh parsley	1-2 tablespoons chopped fresh parsley

Cut the turnips into sticks like potato chips. Drop them into boiling salted water, simmer for 15 minutes or until just tender; be careful not to overcook. Drain and dry them in the colander under a cloth to keep warm. Soften the butter in the hot pan until creamy, but do not allow it to go oily. Add the turnips and then the mustard gradually and stir until the turnips are thoroughly coated. Mix in the chopped parsley and serve very hot.

Carrots

These are available all the year but the young early carrots, which start in April, are the most delicate. They are sold in bunches complete with leaves which must be removed. They only need scrubbing and are casseroled or boiled whole and tossed with chopped fresh mint, chervil or parsley.

Glazed Carrots

METRIC	IMPERIAL
½ kg carrots, scraped	1 lb carrots, scraped
300 ml good White stock (p. 14)	½ pint good White stock (p. 14)
50 g butter	2 oz butter
1 tablespoon granulated sugar	1 tablespoon granulated sugar
salt	salt
freshly ground pepper	freshly ground pepper
chopped mint or parsley	chopped mint or parsley

Cut the carrots into rounds or fingers. Put them in a sauté pan, cover with the stock and add the butter and sugar. Cover the pan, bring quickly to boil and simmer gently for 20 minutes. Remove the lid and continue cooking until the liquid is reduced to a glaze. Stir carefully from time to time to prevent the carrots catching and burning. When they are bright and glistening, season to taste with salt and pepper and place them in a hot serving dish and sprinkle with chopped fresh mint or parsley. If you are keeping them warm in the oven, do not cover the vegetable dish because condensation will spoil the glaze.

Swedes (Swedish Turnips)

These are available from September to May. The golden flesh is slightly sweet and takes longer to cook than white turnips. Choose the smaller roots. Trim, peel and wash and cut in slices or chunks.
Casserole or boil for 45 minutes or so until tender. Drain and dry over low heat. Toss in butter and parsley.

Mashed Swedes

Dry 1 kg/2 lb boiled swedes and mash them thoroughly. Add 2 tablespoons bacon fat or butter and season well with salt and freshly ground pepper. Garnish with chopped parsley.

Skirlie-Mirlie

Add an equal quantity of Mashed potatoes (p. 98) to the mashed swedes. Whip together with a little hot milk and extra bacon fat or butter over low heat until creamy. Season well with salt and freshly ground pepper and serve garnished with chopped fresh parsley.

Parsnips

These are in season from September to April and are best in autumn. Peel and wash. If large, quarter and remove the core. Boil or casserole in the same way as carrots. Parsnips may also be cut into sticks and deep fried as for chips (p. 67).
To roast: Prepare parsnip wedges and boil for 5 to 10 minutes in salted water. Drain and dry and cook in hot fat round the roasting joint for 45 minutes to 1 hour; or roast in a separate tin with hot dripping or lard.

Leaf Vegetables

Brussels Sprouts

In season from August to March. Allow ½ kg/1 lb for 3 to 4 servings.

Choose firm, tight sprouts with fresh green colour. Remove the damaged leaves, trim the stalks and slit them crosswise. Drop into boiling, salted water, just sufficient to cover the sprouts, and simmer for 10 to 15 minutes. Do not overcook. Drain thoroughly. Melt 25 g/1 oz butter for each ½ kg/1 lb sprouts in the warm empty pan and toss until well buttered. Season with salt and freshly ground black pepper and a little nutmeg.

Broccoli

In season all the year. Allow ½ kg/1 lb for 4 servings. There are three different types:—

Purple Sprouting Broccoli

Remove any tough stalks and coarse leaves. Chop roughly, leaving the florets whole; wash well. Cook in boiling salted water for 10 to 15 minutes or until tender, drain thoroughly. Melt butter in a warm empty pan – 4 tablespoons butter per ½ kg/1 lb broccoli – and toss the broccoli in it, seasoning with salt and freshly ground pepper. Alternatively, serve with Poulette sauce (p. 106).

Green Broccoli Spears

Shorten stalks to equal length and wash. Lay the spears in a sauté pan and cover them with boiling, salted water. Simmer very gently for 10 minutes or until tender. Remove with a fish slice and place on a clean cloth or absorbent kitchen paper to drain. Arrange the broccoli spears carefully in a warm serving dish and pour 3-4 tablespoons melted butter over them.

A la Crème

Heat 75 ml/3 fl oz single cream per ½ kg/1 lb broccoli. Season with lemon juice, salt and freshly ground pepper and pour the cream over the cooked broccoli spears.

Au Gratin

Arrange the cooked broccoli spears in a shallow flameproof dish. Pour over 3-4 tablespoons melted butter, sprinkle with grated cheese and flash under a preheated grill.

Cape Broccoli (Calabrese)

In season from July to December. The purple and green heads are similar to cauliflower but are more delicate. Cook as for cauliflower and serve as for broccoli spears with cream or Poulette sauce (p. 106).

Cauliflower

In season all the year round. Select firm white heads with fresh leaves. Trim the stalk and slit it crosswise. Remove any coarse leaves and wash well. Place the cauliflower stem downwards in boiling salted water and simmer for 15 minutes or until it is just tender when tested with a skewer. Carefully place the cooked cauliflower in a colander to drain, cover with a clean cloth to dry and keep it warm. Cauliflower can be served coated with Lemon, Parsley or Cheese sauce (p. 23). It may also be divided into sprigs (florets) in which case cook for 10 minutes only.

Spinach

In season all the year round. Small-leaved summer spinach is best. Allow 1 kg/2 lb spinach for 4 servings. Remove the stalks and tear larger leaves off the central vein. Wash in several changes of cold water to remove grit. Put in a saucepan without water, sprinkle with salt. Cover and cook over low heat for about 10 minutes, according to quantity, shaking the pan occasionally. When cooked, turn the spinach into a colander and drain thoroughly. The quantity will have greatly diminished. Reheat with butter or single cream and season with salt and freshly ground pepper.

Alternatively, put the spinach in a blender and purée, then reheat with butter or cream.

Cauliflower in Parsley Sauce; Green Broccoli Spears au Gratin

Cabbage

In season all the year. Allow ½ kg/1 lb for three to four servings. There are green, white and red varieties. Spring greens, available from November to April, are young cabbages without hearts. They wilt quickly so they must be used very fresh. Spring, summer and winter cabbage with heart, when bought fresh, can be stored for 2 to 3 days in a cool, dark place, or in a plastic bag in the refrigerator. Remove the coarse outer leaves, quarter the heart and shred it after removing the stalk (see facing page), using a large knife or a shredder. Wash in cold water and drain in a colander.

Buttered Cabbage

Put shredded cabbage in a large pan with just enough boiling water to cover the base. Season with salt, cover and cook over low heat, shaking occasionally, for about 10 minutes, until tender but still slightly crisp. Do not overcook. Drain in a colander. For four servings, melt 25 g/1 oz butter in the warm empty saucepan, add the cooked cabbage and stir well, seasoning with salt, freshly ground pepper and a pinch of nutmeg. Serve very hot.

Austrian Cabbage with Soured Cream

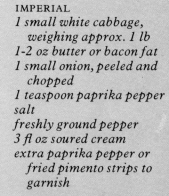

METRIC	IMPERIAL
1 small white cabbage, weighing approx. ½ kg	*1 small white cabbage, weighing approx. 1 lb*
25-50 g butter or bacon fat	*1-2 oz butter or bacon fat*
1 small onion, peeled and chopped	*1 small onion, peeled and chopped*
1 teaspoon paprika pepper	*1 teaspoon paprika pepper*
salt	*salt*
freshly ground pepper	*freshly ground pepper*
100 ml soured cream	*3 fl oz soured cream*
extra paprika pepper or fried pimento strips to garnish	*extra paprika pepper or fried pimento strips to garnish*

Step 1 Remove any discoloured or coarse leaves from the cabbage. Cut the heart into quarters and remove the stalk. Shred finely, wash and drain. Preheat the oven to 160°C, 325°F or gas mark 3.

Step 2 In a flameproof casserole, heat the butter or bacon fat and fry the onion gently until softened. Add the cabbage and sauté lightly until well buttered.

Step 3 Season with paprika pepper, salt and freshly ground pepper. Stir in the soured cream and mix well.

Step 4 Cover with a lid and bake in the oven for 20 minutes, or cook over low heat on top of the stove. Do not overheat or the cream will separate. Garnish with paprika pepper or fried pimento strips. Excellent with Hungarian goulash and grilled pork chops.

Stem Vegetables

Leeks

In season from August to May. Allow 1-2 leeks per serving. Avoid very large ones, except for using in soup.

Step 1 Cut off the roots, and the green tops to within 5 cm/2 inches of the white part. Peel off the outer coarse or discoloured leaves.

Step 2 Cut two slits crosswise through the green leaves down to the white part.

Step 3 Plunge the leek heads up and down in cold water until all the grit is removed.

Step 4 Bring enough salted water to boiling point in a sauté pan to cover the leeks, put them in and simmer for 15 to 25 minutes, according to size, until tender when tested with a skewer. Lift out, and lay on clean cloth to drain, folding cloth over to keep them warm.

Serving Suggestions

Leeks with Sauce

Arrange well drained cooked leeks lengthwise in a warm serving dish and coat with Parsley sauce (p. 23) or Poulette sauce (p. 106).

Cheesey Leeks

Coat the cooked leeks with Cheese sauce (p. 23). Sprinkle generously with grated cheese and brown under the grill.

Leeks au Gratin

Well butter a shallow flameproof dish. Arrange the cooked leeks neatly on the dish, sprinkle them thickly with grated cheese and dot with butter. Cook under the grill until the cheese is bubbling and golden.

Leeks à la Niçoise

Prepare the leeks, trimming off all green leaves. For 4 leeks heat 2 tablespoons olive oil in a flameproof casserole and fry the leeks until slightly coloured, turning them once. Add 1 small can (225 g/8 oz) Italian tomatoes. Add a pinch of basil and flavour to taste with garlic, salt, freshly ground black pepper and sugar.

Cook over low heat for 20 minutes or until tender. Serve sprinkled with chopped parsley.

Braised Celery Hearts; Flemish Chicory with Ham and Cheese Sauce; Leeks with Poulette Sauce

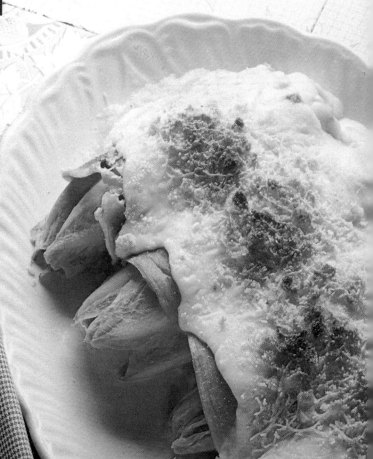

Celery

Available all year round. Allow 1 small head or 3-4 sticks per serving. The main varieties are white blanched celery, self-blanched and unblanched green celery. Select roots with fresh green leaves and smooth sticks. Ridged stalks are coarse so use them for soup and stews; first remove the 'strings' and chop the stalks. Trim off the roots and green tops – the latter may be used as a garnish. Remove coarse or damaged outer stalks. Keep the hearts whole, separate outer stalks, and wash thoroughly.

Celery with Sauce

Cut celery into 5 cm/2 inch lengths and cook in boiling salted water for 10 to 20 minutes, until tender. Drain and use the liquid to make Poulette sauce (p. 106), or use it with 50 per cent milk for Parsley or Cheese sauce (p. 23). Mix the celery in the chosen sauce and garnish with chopped fresh parsley.

Braised Celery Hearts

METRIC	IMPERIAL
4 small or 2 large celery hearts	*4 small or 2 large celery hearts*
300 ml good stock (p. 14) or bouillon	*½ pint good stock (p. 14) or bouillon*
50 g Beurre manié (p. 152)	*2 oz Beurre manié (p. 152)*

Trim and clean the celery. Cut the hearts and stalks down to 10 cm/4 inch lengths. Tie the stalks into small bundles. Place the celery in a casserole and add sufficient stock to cover. Cover with a lid and simmer gently on top of stove or in a preheated oven at 180°C, 350°F or gas mark 4 for 1 hour or until tender.

When the celery is cooked, place it neatly in a warm serving dish. Remove the strings and keep it warm. Add beurre manié one ball at a time to the stock in the casserole, stirring steadily until the sauce is of a creamy consistency. Boil for 3 to 5 minutes to cook the flour thoroughly. Taste and adjust the seasoning and pour the sauce over the celery.

Chicory (Belgian Endive)

In season most of the year. Allow 1 large or 2 small heads per serving. Remove any damaged leaves. Trim the base and, with a pointed knife, dig out the core as it tends to taste bitter. Wash and blanch the heads for 5 minutes in boiling salted water and drain. Simmer in salted water for 20 to 30 minutes, drain and serve in the same way as leeks, or braise as for celery hearts, or Flemish style for a lunch or supper dish, as follows:

Flemish Chicory with Ham and Cheese Sauce

METRIC	IMPERIAL
4 medium chicory heads	*4 medium chicory heads*
4 slices cooked ham	*4 slices cooked ham*
300 ml Cheese sauce (p. 23)	*½ pint Cheese sauce (p. 23)*
3 tablespoons grated cheese	*3 tablespoons grated cheese*
1-2 tablespoons crisp breadcrumbs	*1-2 tablespoons crisp breadcrumbs*

Roll each blanched chicory head in a slice of ham and place in a buttered shallow ovenproof dish. Pour cheese sauce over the chicory and cover with grated cheese and breadcrumbs. Bake in a preheated oven at 190°C, 375°F or gas mark 5 for 20 to 30 minutes, until golden brown and sizzling.

Pod Vegetables

French Beans

Available most of the year, but scarce and expensive in winter. Allow ½ kg/1 lb for four servings. Select young crisp beans which snap easily. Top and tail if necessary. Wash and simmer gently in salted water for 10 to 20 minutes, according to age and size. They should be tender but still crisp. Drain in a colander, then plunge quickly in and out of cold water to refresh the colour. Reheat by tossing in melted butter in a hot saucepan. Arrange the beans neatly in a warm dish, do not tumble them in roughly.

French Beans with Poulette Sauce

METRIC	IMPERIAL
½ kg French beans	1 lb French beans
50 g butter	2 oz butter
1 tablespoon flour	1 tablespoon flour
salt	salt
freshly ground black pepper	freshly ground black pepper
pinch of mixed dried herbs	pinch of mixed dried herbs
1 egg yolk	1 egg yolk
lemon juice	lemon juice
2 tablespoons chopped fresh parsley	2 tablespoons chopped fresh parsley

Prepare and cook the beans as above, drain in a colander and keep warm under a cloth. Reserve the bean liquor. Melt the butter in a small saucepan. Withdraw the pan from the heat, stir in the flour and gradually blend in 300 ml/½ pint of the bean liquor. Bring to the boil, stirring well. Add salt and pepper to taste and the mixed herbs, reduce the heat and simmer gently for 5 to 10 minutes.

Beat the egg yolk with 1 tablespoon lemon juice and 2 tablespoons of the bean liquor. Remove the sauce from the heat and stir in the egg yolk mixture. Reheat without boiling. Taste and adjust the seasoning, adding more lemon juice if desired. Arrange the beans neatly in a warm serving dish, pour the sauce over them and sprinkle with chopped fresh parsley.

Tuscan French Beans
Follow the recipe for Runner beans Tuscan style (opposite) but leave the beans whole.

Green Peas à la Française; French Beans with Poulette Sauce; Runner Beans Tuscan Style

Bobby Beans

These are similar to French beans, but round instead of flat. They are topped and tailed and cooked and served in the same ways as French beans. They are usually cheaper to buy.

Broad Beans

These are in season from April to September. When they are very young and the beans inside the pods are immature, first top and tail them, then chop them across as for runner beans and cook and serve in the same way.

When mature, remove the beans from the pods, simmer for 15-20 minutes in salted water and drain. Toss them in butter with chopped fresh parsley or sage or serve them in Parsley sauce (p. 23) or Poulette sauce made with the bean liquor. When the beans are very large, remove the skins after boiling and sieve them or purée them in a blender; add butter and season well with salt and pepper.

Runner Beans

In season from mid-July to October. Allow ½ kg/1 lb per four servings. Runner beans are much larger than French beans, but select young ones which snap easily. Top and tail them and remove the strings from the sides with a small vegetable knife. Cut the beans obliquely into chunks 2½ cm/1 inch long, French style. In England they are often shredded, but this reduces the flavour and vitamin C. Simmer in salted water for 10 minutes or until tender. Drain in a colander and toss in melted butter in a warm saucepan. Season with salt and freshly ground pepper and flavour with chopped fresh parsley or sage.

Runner Beans with Poulette Sauce

Prepare, cook and drain as above, reserve liquor and follow the recipe for French beans with Poulette sauce.

Runner Beans Tuscan Style

METRIC	IMPERIAL
½ kg runner beans	1 lb runner beans
50 g butter	2 oz butter
1 tablespoon olive oil	1 tablespoon olive oil
2 tablespoons chopped fresh sage or parsley or 1 teaspoon dried sage	2 tablespoons chopped fresh sage or parsley or 1 teaspoon dried sage
1 clove garlic, crushed	1 clove garlic, crushed
salt	salt
freshly ground pepper	freshly ground pepper
¼ teaspoon ground nutmeg	¼ teaspoon ground nutmeg
1 tablespoon grated Parmesan cheese	1 tablespoon grated Parmesan cheese

Prepare, cook and drain the beans as above. Heat the butter and oil in a saucepan, stir in 1 tablespoon of the sage or parsley and the crushed garlic and fry for 1 minute. Add the cooked beans, season to taste with salt and pepper and add the nutmeg. Stir over gentle heat for 5 minutes. Mix in the grated cheese and serve at once sprinkled with the remaining fresh herbs.

Mange Tout (Sugar Peas)

These have flat pods containing small, undeveloped peas and are cooked and eaten whole in the pods. Select young fresh peas, top and tail the pods and string if necessary. Simmer gently in salted water, drain and toss in butter and chopped fresh herbs if liked.

Green Peas

In season May to October. Allow 1 kg/2 lb peas in the pod for four servings. Select peas with crisp shiny pods which are well filled. Young peas, called petits pois, are very tender and sweet. Shell, just cover with boiling water, add salt, a teaspoon of sugar and a sprig of fresh mint. Simmer very gently for 10 minutes for small peas, 15 to 20 minutes for large peas. Drain and toss with butter. Mature peas are better casseroled as in the following recipe:

Green Peas à la Française

METRIC	IMPERIAL
1 kg peas, shelled	2 lbs peas, shelled
25 g butter	1 oz butter
1 rasher streaky bacon, de-rinded and chopped	1 rasher streaky bacon, de-rinded and chopped
4 spring onions, chopped	4 spring onions, chopped
¼ lettuce	¼ lettuce
1 teaspoon sugar	1 teaspoon sugar
salt	salt
freshly ground pepper	freshly ground pepper
fresh mint	fresh mint

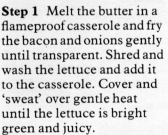

Step 1 Melt the butter in a flameproof casserole and fry the bacon and onions gently until transparent. Shred and wash the lettuce and add it to the casserole. Cover and 'sweat' over gentle heat until the lettuce is bright green and juicy.

Step 2 Tip in the peas, add a sprig of mint, sugar and salt and pepper to taste. Cover and cook over gentle heat on top of the stove for 30 minutes, or in the oven at 150°C, 300°F or gas mark 2 for 45 minutes or until tender.

Replace the cooked mint with fresh sprigs to garnish.

Gourds

Vegetable Marrow

In season July to October. Select young marrows up to 30 cm/12 inches long. As they mature, the flesh becomes tough and tasteless. They have a high water content so should not be boiled, but casseroled, baked, or deep fried in batter.

To casserole: Cut the marrow into slices 2.5 cm/1 inch thick, peel and cut into wedges, discarding the seeds. Well butter a casserole, put in the marrow chunks, season each layer with salt and freshly ground black pepper, and sprinkle with fresh green herbs – parsley, chervil and chives, together or singly. Dot generously with butter, cover and cook very gently over low heat, shaking occasionally, or in the oven at 150°C, 300°F or gas mark 2 for 20 to 30 minutes, until tender but not too soft.

To bake or roast: Cut the marrow into thick slices and peel. Cut the slices in half across and remove the seeds. Toss the pieces in flour and roast in hot fat round the joint or in a separate baking tin. Season with salt and freshly ground pepper when serving.

Marrow Fritters

Cut a peeled marrow into small chunks and remove the seeds. Spread the chunks on kitchen paper and sprinkle with salt. Dry on absorbent kitchen paper, dip in coating batter and fry in deep fat (see Fruit fritters, p. 81). Serve immediately.

Back row: shallots; Spanish onions. Front row: pickling onions; maincrop English onions; crispy fried onions

Courgettes

These are a small variety of vegetable marrow and are available all the year. Use them when fresh as they acquire a bitter taste if kept. Select courgettes about 15 cm/6 inches long. Top and tail them, but do not peel or remove the seeds. Cut in rounds and casserole with herbs, sauté in butter or deep fry in batter as for marrow (but do not peel).

Courgettes au Gratin

Step 1 Top, tail and wipe 4 courgettes and cut them in half lengthwise. Heat 50 g/2 oz butter in a shallow flameproof casserole and fry the courgette halves cut side down until golden.

Step 2 Turn the courgettes over, season with salt and freshly ground pepper. Sprinkle with grated cheese, dot with butter. Put on a lid and cook gently on top of the stove for 20 minutes, or in the oven at 180°C, 350°F or gas mark 4 for 30 minutes or until tender. Trickle a little hot cream over the courgettes, flash under a hot grill and serve at once. These courgettes freeze and reheat very successfully, but add the cream after reheating.

Bulbs

Onions

There are many varieties of onion. The maincrop English onion is in season from September to March. If they are of good quality, they store well in cool dry conditions. The large sweet onion with a mild flavour is called Spanish, but this variety is not confined to Spain. The small pickling onions and white button onions are available from July to October. The thin little 'spring' or salad onions are available all the year, but are scarce in winter. Shallots grow in little clumps and are small, white and are used for delicate dishes.

To boil: Trim the tops and cut off the root end then peel off all the brown skin. Cook in boiling salted water for 30 to 45 minutes, according to size, or until tender. Drain well and serve covered with Parsley or Cheese sauce (p. 23) if liked.

To fry (sauté): Skin and slice the onions. Heat sufficient lard or oil to cover the base of the frying pan and fry the onions slowly until they are golden brown and soft. Stir frequently, season with salt and freshly ground pepper and serve very hot.

Crispy Fried Onions

Skin, slice and break the onions into rings. Deep fry in Light continental batter (p. 80).

To roast: Top and tail Spanish onions and wipe the brown skins. Cover the base of a roasting pan with greased foil. Put in the onions and bake in a preheated oven at 200°C, 400°F or gas mark 6 for 1 hour, or longer if the onions are large. When the onions are tender, move them to a warm serving dish, remove the skins, open the centre and season with salt and freshly ground pepper. Push in a knob of butter and top with a sprig of parsley.

Glazed Onions

Skin and cook pickling or button onions in boiling salted water for 20 minutes or until tender. Drain and dry on absorbent kitchen paper. Heat enough butter in a sauté pan to cover the base of the pan, add the onions and sprinkle them with caster sugar. Cook over gentle heat, shaking frequently, until they glaze. Serve with the rest of the butter and sugar poured over and sprinkle with chopped parsley.

Glazed onions; boiled onions in parsley sauce; roast onions

Pulses

Pulse is the general term for the dried edible seeds from the pods of leguminous plants. They are a valuable source of protein and in many countries pulses are used to replace or extend meat. They include butter beans, haricot beans, red kidney beans, whole or split peas, chick peas and brown, green and red lentils. With the exception of red lentils, they need to be soaked before cooking to restore their moisture.

Cover the beans or lentils with boiling water and soak overnight. Throw the soaking water away, as it tends to ferment, and use fresh water for cooking. Do not add salt to the cooking water until the pulses start to get tender as salt retards softening.

Buy pulses where there is a frequent turnover, as those which have been long in store remain hard even after long slow cooking, though cooking in a pressure cooker will help to soften them. They swell considerably as they absorb water and nearly treble in bulk, so 50 g/2 oz per serving is usually sufficient.

Butter Beans with Sauce

Soak the beans as described and drain. Cover generously with cold water, bring to the boil, cover and simmer for 1 hour or until tender, adding salt towards the end of cooking. Drain and measure off 300 ml/½ pint of the bean liquor. Use this to make Parsley, Onion or Cheese sauce (p. 23) and mix in the drained beans. For a rich sauce, reduce amount of bean liquor and add 4 tablespoons cream. These are good with grilled ham or bacon, sausages, lamb or pork chops.

Boston Baked Beans; Fried Mexican Beans; Pease Pudding; Lentils with Parsley Butter

Boston Baked Beans

METRIC	IMPERIAL
225 g-350 g haricot beans, soaked overnight	*8-12 oz haricot beans, soaked overnight*
2 medium onions, peeled and chopped	*2 medium onions, peeled and chopped*
100 g salt pork, diced	*4 oz salt pork, diced*
2 tablespoons treacle or dark brown sugar	*2 tablespoons treacle or dark brown sugar*
2-3 tablespoons tomato ketchup	*2-3 tablespoons tomato ketchup*
1 tablespoon cider vinegar	*1 tablespoon cider vinegar*
1 teaspoon dry mustard	*1 teaspoon dry mustard*
1 teaspoon salt	*1 teaspoon salt*
1 tablespoon Worcester sauce (optional)	*1 tablespoon Worcester sauce (optional)*

Drain the soaked beans and simmer them in fresh water for about 1 hour. To test, take out a few beans on a spoon; if when you blow on them the skins burst, they are ready. Drain them, reserving the liquor. Put the beans in a greased casserole. Mix in the other ingredients and just enough liquid to cover them. Put on a lid and bake in a preheated oven at 150°C, 300°F or gas mark 2 for 7 to 8 hours. Stir occasionally and leave uncovered for the last hour. If the beans become too dry, add a little more liquid.

Fried Mexican Beans

METRIC	IMPERIAL
225 g red kidney beans, soaked overnight	8 oz red kidney beans, soaked overnight
100 g onions, peeled and coarsely chopped	4 oz onions, peeled and coarsely chopped
1 × 225 g can tomatoes	1 × 8 oz can tomatoes
salt	salt
50 g lard	2 oz lard
1 clove garlic, finely chopped	1 clove garlic, finely chopped
¼ teaspoon chilli powder	¼ teaspoon chilli powder
freshly ground pepper	freshly ground pepper

Drain the soaked beans and put them in a large thick pan with 1 tablespoon of the onion, 2 tablespoons of the tomatoes and sufficient fresh water to cover the beans. Bring to the simmer and cook gently for 1 hour or until the beans start to soften. Add salt to taste and a knob of lard. Continue cooking for a further 30 minutes or until the beans are completely soft, stirring from time to time as the liquid is absorbed. Withdraw the pan from the heat. In a large thick frying pan, heat the remaining lard and fry the rest of the onions and the garlic until transparent. Stir in the rest of the tomatoes and simmer for 2 to 3 minutes. Gradually add the cooked beans, mashing them as you go. Add the chilli powder (not too much as it is very hot) and salt and pepper to taste. Cook gently over low heat, stirring steadily until the mixture thickens. Turn the fried beans into a heated bowl and serve with fried or baked chorizo (smoked Spanish sausage) or spicy pork sausages.

Pease Pudding

METRIC	IMPERIAL
225 g split peas, soaked overnight	8 oz split peas, soaked overnight
1 ham bone or bacon scraps	1 ham bone or bacon scraps
1 onion, peeled and spiked with cloves	1 onion, peeled and spiked with cloves
25 g butter	1 oz butter
1 egg, beaten	1 egg, beaten
pinch of sugar	pinch of sugar
salt	salt
freshly ground pepper	freshly ground pepper
parsley sprigs to garnish	parsley sprigs to garnish

Drain the soaked peas and tie in a loose muslin cloth allowing room for them to swell. Put them in a saucepan and cover with cold water. Add the ham bone and onion. Simmer for 2 hours or until soft. Lift out the bag, put the peas through a mouli or sieve and add the butter, egg, sugar and salt and pepper to taste. Beat the ingredients together well and tie up tightly in a floured cloth. Return the pudding to the pan and simmer for a further 30 minutes. Turn the pudding into a warm serving bowl and garnish with parsley. Serve very hot. This goes well with baked or boiled ham or a bacon joint.

Lentils with Parsley Butter

METRIC	IMPERIAL
225 g brown or green lentils, soaked for 1 hour	8 oz brown or green lentils, soaked for 1 hour
250 ml good White or Brown stock (p. 14, 16)	8 fl oz good White or Brown stock (p. 14, 16)
40 g Parsley butter (p. 153)	1½ oz Parsley butter (p. 153)

Drain the soaked lentils, cover with cold water and simmer for 1 hour or until they are tender. If the water is not absorbed, strain the lentils, add the stock and cook gently until no liquid remains.

Remove the pan from the heat, stir in the parsley butter and season to taste with salt and pepper. Serve with sausages, roast pork or game.

Salads

Salads can be made entirely with raw ingredients, or with all cooked ingredients, or with a mixture of both. They can be served as side dishes, or as an hors d'oeuvre, or – combined with fish, chicken or meat – as a main dish. The dressing can vary in texture and richness, as well as in flavour. Lettuce and watercress must be dressed at the last minute or the leaves will wilt. Tomatoes, cucumber, potatoes and beans are improved if marinated in the dressing for half an hour or longer. Crisp shredded cabbage, too, can be dressed and chilled in advance of serving.

Tossed Green Salad

Lettuce is the basis of this salad. The round cabbage lettuce is available all the year round. There are two types, the soft leaved variety and the crisp Webbs Wonder with its tightly curled, compact heart. The tall Cos lettuce, with its sweet tasting leaves and crisp heart, is at its best in the summer.

With the exception of the cabbage-like heart of the Webbs, lettuce leaves should be torn in pieces, not cut with a knife. Discard any coarse outer leaves, wash the rest carefully and dry by swinging in a salad basket or using a salad spinner. Arrange the lettuce in a salad bowl with sprigs of watercress, which is available all year, but tastes peppery when in flower. Cut off the coarse watercress stalks, wash and dry the sprigs.

Tender leaves from the hearts of curly endive can also be added, or some small chicory leaves. Just before serving, toss the salad with a few tablespoons of well mixed French dressing opposite. Serve with cold dishes, hot roast poultry and game, grills, cheese soufflé and pasta dishes.

Mixed French Salad

Prepare salad as above and add some sliced cucumber, tomato wedges and crisp radishes which have been washed, topped and tailed. Trim and peel a few fresh spring onions, leave them 2 or 3 inches long or chop up the white part and sprinkle it over the salad. Toss with French dressing.

Cucumber and Tomato Salad

Top and tail half a cucumber, wipe it and peel if preferred. Cut it into thin slices. Wipe 4 tomatoes and slice them across, not downwards. Arrange the cucumber and tomatoes in overlapping slices in a round shallow flat dish. Pour over 3-4 tablespoons well mixed French dressing. Sprinkle with chopped fresh green herbs – tarragon, chives, mint, chervil or parsley, singly or mixed. Leave to marinate for 30 minutes before serving.

Mixed French Salad; Rosy Winter Salad; Salad Niçoise

Potato Salad

Wash and boil new or small maincrop potatoes until just cooked (p. 96). Peel them, then slice or cut into dice. Mix in French dressing (opposite) carefully while the potatoes are still warm. Sprinkle with chopped spring onions and fresh herbs. Marinate for 30 minutes or longer and serve in a bowl lined with lettuce or curly endive leaves. Mayonnaise (p. 28) may be used instead of French dressing.

Rosy Winter Salad

METRIC	IMPERIAL
150 ml Sour cream dressing (see opposite)	*¼ pint Sour cream dressing (see opposite)*
2-3 heads chicory	*2-3 heads chicory*
1-2 celery hearts	*1-2 celery hearts*
1 small cooked beetroot	*1 small cooked beetroot*
3 rosy dessert apples	*3 rosy dessert apples*
lemon juice	*lemon juice*
walnut halves to garnish (optional)	*walnut halves to garnish (optional)*

Trim off chicory stems and discard any discoloured leaves. Set aside some outside leaves to line the salad bowl and chop the remainder. Wash and chop the celery heart, retaining some leaves for garnish. Push skin and root off the beetroot with the thumbs. Cut out some balls with a French scoop and set aside for garnish. Dice remaining beetroot. Peel, core and dice 2 of the apples and mix quickly into the salad dressing. Add prepared chicory, celery and diced beetroot, stir until well blended. Spoon the salad into the salad bowl lined with chicory leaves. Cut remaining unpeeled apple into wedges, rub with lemon juice and arrange as petals in centre of the salad. Arrange beetroot balls and walnut halves around the apple and garnish with a tuft of young celery leaves.

Coleslaw

This salad of Dutch-American origin is usually made with the white Dutch cabbage, but red cabbage is also very good. Prepare ½ kg/1 lb cabbage heart and shred it finely (p. 103). Crisp in cold water and drain thoroughly.

Mix the cabbage with 150 ml/¼ pint Sour cream mayonnaise, i.e. equal quantities of Mayonnaise (p. 28) and soured cream. Add chopped apple, peppers, celery seed and paprika pepper if liked. Season to taste.

Salad Niçoise

METRIC	IMPERIAL
225 g tomatoes	8 oz tomatoes
½ Spanish onion	½ Spanish onion
1 small or ½ large green pepper	1 small or ½ large green pepper
1 lettuce heart	1 lettuce heart
1 × 90 g can tuna fish	1 × 3½ oz can tuna fish
6 anchovy fillets	6 anchovy fillets
75 ml Garlic French dressing	3 fl oz Garlic French dressing
225 g French beans, cooked	8 oz French beans, cooked
6 black olives, stoned	6 black olives, stoned
2 hard-boiled eggs	2 hard-boiled eggs

Skin the tomatoes and cut into quarters. Peel and slice the onion and break it into rings. Halve the pepper, remove stem and seeds and finely slice the flesh. Wash and dry the lettuce. Drain the tuna fish and flake it roughly. Split the anchovy fillets lengthwise. Shell and quarter the eggs.

Put half the French dressing in a shallow salad bowl and toss in it the prepared lettuce and beans. Arrange the tuna fish on top with the onion rings, peppers and olives, and the hard-boiled eggs topped with anchovy fillets. Sprinkle with the remaining dressing. This salad makes an attractive first course when served on individual plates.

Sour Cream Dressing

METRIC	IMPERIAL
150 ml soured cream	¼ pint soured cream
or	or
150 ml thick cream mixed with 1 tablespoon lemon juice	¼ pint thick cream mixed with 1 tablespoon lemon juice
1 teaspoon French mustard	1 teaspoon French mustard
1-2 teaspoons caster sugar	1-2 teaspoons caster sugar
salt	salt
freshly ground black pepper	freshly ground black pepper
lemon juice	lemon juice

Mix the ingredients thoroughly, season to taste with salt, pepper and lemon juice.

French Dressing (Sauce Vinaigrette)

This dressing keeps well so you can mix up at least 300 ml/½ pint and store it in a screw top jar; this will prevent evaporation and enable you to shake it up before use. The proportion of oil to vinegar can be varied, but the vinegar, plain or tarragon flavoured, should be wine or cider based; not coarse malt vinegar. Olive oil gives the best flavour but it can be mixed or replaced with corn oil.

METRIC	IMPERIAL
½ teaspoon salt	½ teaspoon salt
½ teaspoon caster sugar	½ teaspoon caster sugar
½ teaspoon French mustard	½ teaspoon French mustard
¼ teaspoon ground black pepper	¼ teaspoon ground black pepper
75 ml wine or cider vinegar	3 fl oz wine or cider vinegar
150 ml olive oil	6 fl oz olive oil

Mix all seasonings together and stir in the vinegar. Mix in the oil and whip or shake well to blend thoroughly. Taste and adjust the seasoning if wished.

Lemon French Dressing
Use lemon juice instead of vinegar.

Fresh Herb Dressing
Add 1-2 tablespoons chopped fresh tarragon, chives, chervil or mint.

Rice   Types of rice

There are several varieties of rice such as white polished rice, brown unpolished rice and wild rice. There are also various types of processed rice, which should be cooked according to the manufacturer's instructions.

The white and brown rice are both available in three sizes of grain – long for serving with savoury dishes, medium and short for stuffings and puddings. Wild rice is scarce and expensive and takes a long time to cook. Rice trebles in bulk when cooked. Allow 40-50 g/1½-2 oz per serving.

To Boil White Rice

Put plenty of water in a large saucepan, allowing ½ litre/1 pint water and 1 teaspoon salt to each 50 g/2 oz rice. Add a little lemon juice to whiten the rice and add flavour. Bring the water to the boil, trickle in the rice and boil briskly for 12 to 14 minutes, until just tender. Do not overcook – the texture should be slightly nutty. Stir occasionally to prevent the rice sticking to the bottom of the pan. When ready, drain it in a colander or sieve, then place it over the empty hot saucepan and cover the rice with a crumpled dry cloth to absorb steam and keep the rice hot. After 10 minutes, stir the bottom rice to the top and re-cover until required. This simple method, which boils off the surplus starch into the ample water, makes it unnecessary to wash the rice before cooking or refresh it in cold water afterwards. It will be warm, dry and fluffy. Serve it with curry, or with a succulent casserole instead of potatoes, or use it to make an attractive border to a well-sauced fish, poultry or meat dish.

Kedgeree; Risotto Espagnole

Kedgeree

METRIC	IMPERIAL
350-450 g smoked cod or haddock fillet	*12-16 oz smoked cod or haddock fillet*
75 g butter	*3 oz butter*
225 g long-grain rice, boiled	*8 oz long-grain rice, boiled*
2 hard-boiled eggs	*2 hard-boiled eggs*
3 tablespoons chopped parsley	*3 tablespoons chopped parsley*
lemon juice to taste	*lemon juice to taste*
salt	*salt*
freshly ground black pepper	*freshly ground black pepper*
lemon butterflies to garnish	*lemon butterflies to garnish*

Poach the fish (p. 74), remove any skin and bones and flake the flesh. Heat the butter in a large frying pan and stir in the cooked rice and flaked fish. Chop and add one hard-boiled egg and 1½ tablespoons of the chopped parsley. Sharpen with lemon juice and season well with salt and pepper. Separate the yolk and white of the remaining egg; chop the white and sieve the yolk. Turn the kedgeree into a warm serving dish and decorate with lines of sieved yolk, chopped white and the remaining chopped parsley. Garnish with lemon butterflies. Cooked salmon, fresh or canned, makes an excellent kedgeree.

To Fry Rice

The basis of a risotto is raw rice fried in hot fat with onion. Then it is simmered in stock until the rice is cooked and all the liquid is absorbed. Grated cheese is then added. A simple risotto can be served as a side dish. A more elaborate one – containing shellfish, chicken or meat – makes a main course.

Risotto Espagnole

METRIC	IMPERIAL
50 g butter or 2 tablespoons olive oil	2 oz butter or 2 tablespoons olive oil
1 large onion, peeled and sliced	1 large onion, peeled and sliced
225 g long-grain rice	8 oz long-grain rice
225 ml tomato juice	½ pint tomato juice
stock or bouillon (made with a cube) as required	stock or bouillon (made with a cube) as required
75 g grated cheese	3 oz grated cheese
1 tablespoon paprika pepper	1 teaspoon paprika pepper
salt	salt
freshly ground black pepper	freshly ground black pepper
lemon juice to taste	lemon juice to taste

Step 1 Heat the butter or oil and fry the sliced onion until transparent, stirring steadily. Do not allow it to colour or it will burn when you are frying the rice. Add unwashed rice and stir over moderate heat until it turns a pale biscuit colour; do not brown.

Step 2 Add enough tomato juice to float the rice. Cover and cook over low heat, adding more juice as it is absorbed. Stir frequently to prevent rice sticking. When tomato juice is finished, add stock as needed until rice is cooked and liquid absorbed. The rice should still have a slight bite. If too liquid, cook uncovered until stock has evaporated.

Step 3 Remove the pan from the heat, mix in the grated cheese and stir until it has melted. Season to taste with paprika pepper, salt and pepper. Sharpen to taste with lemon juice. It can now be served as a side dish; for a main course proceed to Step 4.

Step 4 Mix in one of the following: 175-225 g/6-8 oz shelled prawns, smoked sausage, cooked chicken giblets, chopped cooked ham or poultry meat; 100 g/4 oz fried sliced mushroom may also be added. Garnish with cooked green peas or strips of blanched green pepper.

Risotto Milanaise
Replace the tomato juice with good chicken stock (p. 14). When the rice is cooked, mix in ¼ teaspoon (1 packet/12.5 cgs) powdered saffron and add 2-3 tablespoons dry white wine.

Pasta

Pasta is made from a flour and water dough kneaded into a paste which is rolled out thinly, then cut and dried. Homemade pasta is usually enriched with egg. Commercially made pasta is rolled and cut or moulded by machine and dried by a special process. The best pasta is made from hard durum wheat semolina and keeps its shape well during cooking.

Like rice, pasta must be cooked in plenty of boiling, well-salted water. Allow 50 g/2 oz for each serving as an accompanying vegetable (double for Italian guests) and 600 ml/1 pint water and 1 teaspoon salt to each 50 g/2 oz pasta. Bring the water to the boil and drop in the pasta shapes or short-cut macaroni. If using long spaghetti, gradually coil it into the saucepan, do not break it. Simmer uncovered for 10 to 12 minutes, stirring occasionally. The pasta is ready when it begins to look opaque (a small piece may also be tested by tasting). Never overcook or it will be mushy. Drain it in a colander. For 225 g/8 oz pasta, melt 25 g/1 oz butter in the warm saucepan, or heat 1 tablespoon oil, and mix in the drained pasta. Season well with freshly ground pepper and a pinch of nutmeg.

Coiling spaghetti into a pan of simmering water

Serving Suggestions

To serve with fish: Mix in 1 teaspoon grated lemon rind and 1-2 tablespoons chopped fresh parsley.
To serve with veal: Mix in 1 tablespoon chopped chives and 1-2 tablespoons chopped fresh tarragon or parsley.
To serve with beef: Mix in 300 ml/½ pint Tomato sauce.

Egg Noodles Milanaise Style

This is a favourite first course in Italy. Cook 225 g/8 oz egg noodles (tagliatelle) and drain well. Mix with 50 g/2 oz melted butter and 25 g/1 oz grated Parmesan cheese. Stir in 2-3 tablespoons double cream and season well with freshly ground pepper.

Tomato Sauce

METRIC	IMPERIAL
50 g butter or 1 tablespoon olive oil	*2 oz butter or 1 tablespoon olive oil*
1 medium onion, peeled and chopped	*1 medium onion, peeled and chopped*
1 stalk celery, chopped	*1 stalk celery, chopped*
1 × 65 g can tomato purée	*1 × 2½ oz can tomato purée*
1-2 tablespoons flour	*1-2 tablespoons flour*
120 ml red wine	*4 fl oz red wine*
300 ml stock	*½ pint stock*
pinch each of dried basil and marjoram	*pinch each of dried basil and marjoram*
2 teaspoons sugar	*2 teaspoons sugar*
lemon juice	*lemon juice*
salt	*salt*
freshly ground black pepper	*freshly ground black pepper*

Heat the butter or oil and fry the chopped vegetables until they begin to change colour. Add the tomato purée and fry for 2 to 3 minutes, stirring well. Remove from the heat and blend in enough flour to absorb the fat. Gradually stir in the wine and stock and add the herbs. Bring to the boil, stirring, add the sugar and season with salt, pepper and lemon juice. Reduce the heat and simmer for 20 minutes, until the sauce has reduced.

Tagliatelle alla Bolognese

METRIC	IMPERIAL
25 g butter	1 oz butter
50 g bacon or ham, chopped	2 oz bacon or ham, chopped
1 small onion, peeled and chopped	1 small onion, peeled and chopped
1 stalk celery, chopped	1 stalk celery, chopped
50 g mushrooms, washed and sliced	2 oz mushrooms, washed and sliced
100 g minced beef	4 oz minced beef
50 g chicken livers, chopped	2 oz chicken livers, chopped
1 tablespoon tomato purée	1 tablespoon tomato purée
120 ml stock	4 fl oz stock
pinch of dried basil or marjoram	pinch of dried basil or marjoram
1 teaspoon sugar	1 teaspoon sugar
pinch of nutmeg	pinch of nutmeg
salt	salt
freshly ground pepper	freshly ground pepper
225 g tagliatelle	8 oz tagliatelle

Step 1 Melt the butter in a saucepan and fry the bacon, onion, celery and mushrooms gently until softened. Add the minced beef and chicken livers and fry, stirring well, until nicely browned.

Step 2 Add the tomato purée and fry for a minute or two. Stir in the wine and stock. Add the herbs, sugar, nutmeg and salt and pepper to taste. Bring to the simmer, cover and cook gently for 30 to 40 minutes.

Step 3 When the sauce is ready, cook the tagliatelle (see facing page) and drain it well. Lift it into a warm serving bowl with wooden pasta forks.

Step 4 Spoon the bolognese sauce into the centre of the tagliatelle. Hand the grated Parmesan cheese separately and serve with a tossed green salad (p. 112).

Different types of pasta, back row: tagliatelle and tagliatelle verde. Middle row: Rigatoni; ribbon noodles; pasta shells; vermicelli. Front row: Cut and uncut macaroni; lasagne and lasagne verde; cannelloni; spaghetti

Puddings Fruit Salads

A fruit salad can be made at any time of the year, using the fresh fruits in season, and in winter with canned or dried fruit, mixing the colours to give an attractive appearance. It is important to make the syrup before peeling and slicing the fresh fruit as many of them quickly discolour and must be dropped into the syrup as soon as they are prepared.

Fruit Salad; Fruit Compôte

Fruit Compôte

This is made with fruit which has been gently poached in syrup until it is just tender but still holding its shape – not stewed in water into an unappetizing mush. The fruit can be mixed, or all of one kind. The syrup may be flavoured with a stick of cinnamon, or a sliver of lemon or orange rind, or a vanilla pod. If you are using dried fruit – apple rings, pear halves, apricots and prunes – soak the fruit overnight in cold water and use the liquor for the syrup.

Slicing apples

Removing plum stones

Extracting grape pips

Cutting orange into segments

Making pineapple wedges

Scooping out melon balls

To prepare fruit for salad or compôte

Apples and Pears: Peel, quarter and core the apples and slice them immediately into syrup. Rosy apples can be left unpeeled to give colour to the salad.

Plums, Greengages, Apricots: Wash the fruit and remove the stalks. Cut the fruit round its natural crease, twist the two halves in opposite directions and the fruit will split, exposing the stone which is easily removed. Drop the fruit immediately into syrup.

Peaches: Plunge the peaches into boiling water for 2 to 3 minutes and peel. Remove the stone as for plums. Quarter or slice each peach and drop into syrup immediately.

Cherries: Remove the stalks and wash the cherries. Remove stones with a cherry stoner.

Grapes: Split grapes down one side and remove the pips, or leave whole and push a paper clip into the stem end to extract the pips.

Strawberries, Raspberries, Loganberries, Cultivated Blackberries: Remove the stalks and hulls. Rinse carefully in cold water.

Bananas: Peel, slice and drop immediately into syrup.

Oranges, Tangerines, Grapefruit: Put the fruit on a plate to catch the juice. Remove the peel and pith together, sawing downwards with a sharp knife. Hold the fruit firmly and cut down to the centre on either side of the membrane of each segment and remove the flesh. Put segments and juice in the salad bowl.

Pineapple: Cut the pineapple across in thick slices; cut off the rind and remove centre core with an apple corer. Cut the rings into wedges.

Melon: Cut the melon in half and discard the seeds. Scoop the flesh out into balls with a French scoop, or cut it out in small chunks. Drop the pieces into syrup. The empty shell can be used as a basket in which to serve fruit salad. Van dyke (that is, cut 'V' shapes) the edges with a sharp knife.

Syrup for Fruit Salad or Compôte

METRIC	IMPERIAL
225-350 g granulated sugar	8-12 oz granulated sugar
600 ml water	1 pint water
thin sliver of lemon or orange rind	thin sliver of lemon or orange rind
1 vanilla pod (optional)	1 vanilla pod (optional)

Put the sugar in a pan, add the water and lemon or orange rind and the vanilla pod, if used. Bring slowly to the simmer, stirring until sugar is dissolved. When the sugar has completely dissolved, boil briskly without a lid for 5 minutes, or until syrupy. Pour the syrup into a bowl to cool and remove the rind and vanilla pod.

Fruit Purées

When fruit is plentiful and inexpensive, it is a good time to make purées for puddings and cold desserts, as you need about 1 kg/2 lb of fruit to produce 600 ml/1 pint of purée. It is an excellent way to use the windfalls if you have your own fruit trees. Fruit purées freeze very successfully, so it is worth making large quantities if you have a freezer.

Raw fruit purées are quickly made with the soft berry fruits, strawberries, raspberries, loganberries and blackberries. Put through a mouli to remove seeds, sweeten to taste and use for fruit fools, moulds, ice cream and sorbets. Ripe bananas, thoroughly crushed with a fork, sharpened with lemon juice and sweetened to taste with caster sugar, also make a good fool.

Fruit Fool

This can be made with raw or cooked purée mixed with an equal quantity of whipped cream or custard, or half of each. The custard can be made with eggs (p. 30) or custard powder, but as it must be very thick and would need a double quantity of egg yolk, it is more convenient and less expensive to use custard powder or ready-prepared custard. To improve the colour of gooseberry fool, add a few drops of green colouring; for rhubarb fool, add a little cochineal.

Raspberry Fool

METRIC	IMPERIAL
150 ml ready-prepared custard or 1 tablespoon custard powder and 150 ml milk	*¼ pint ready-prepared custard or 1 tablespoon custard powder and ¼ pint milk*
300 ml raspberry purée caster sugar	*½ pint raspberry purée caster sugar*
150 ml whipping cream	*¼ pint whipping cream*
TO GARNISH	TO GARNISH
chopped pistachio nuts or flaked almonds	*chopped pistachio nuts or flaked almonds*

If using custard powder, mix to a thin paste with a little of the cold milk. Boil up the remaining milk and pour it onto the custard, stirring well. Return the custard to the pan and cook for 1 minute, stirring until it thickens. Cool the custard and mix in the fruit purée. Sweeten to taste with caster sugar. Whip the cream stiffly and fold it into the cold fruit mixture. Pour the fool into individual glasses and top with chopped pistachio nuts or flaked almonds. Serve with lady fingers or crisp petits fours biscuits.

Cooked Fruit Purées

To produce a thick, well-flavoured purée, use as little water as possible for cooking and leave the pan uncovered for the last 10 minutes so the liquid evaporates. Stir from time to time to prevent the purée sticking to the pan.

Alternatively, cook the fruit in a casserole in the oven at 180 °C, 350 °F or gas mark 4, until mushy. Do not add sugar until the fruit is cooked as it hardens the skins. The fruit can be mashed complete with skins, very rapidly in an electric blender, or more slowly by hand with a kichamajig or wooden spoon. If you want to eliminate pips, use a mouli (p. 20) as sieving is rather wasteful as well as slow.
Apricots, Greengages, Plums: Wash the fruit and remove stalks and stones (p. 119). Cover the base of a thick pan thinly with water, put in the fruit, cover and cook gently until the juice runs. Remove the lid and continue cooking until the fruit is mushy. Purée and sweeten to taste while still hot.

Danish Apple Crunch; Raspberry Fool

Apples: Quarter, peel and core the apples and remove any damaged flesh. Slice the apples into a bowl of cold water which has a little lemon juice added to prevent the apples discolouring. Grease the bottom of a thick pan with a buttery paper and add 2-3 tablespoons water. Put in the apples, cover and cook gently until the juice begins to flow. Remove the lid and continue cooking gently, stirring occasionally, until the apples are mushy. Beat smooth with a kichamajig or wooden spoon. Sweeten to taste.

Blackberries, Blackcurrants, Gooseberries, Redcurrants: Remove stalks, wash the fruit and cook as for apricots. When cooked, put through a mouli or coarse sieve.

Rhubarb: Cut off leaves, which contain oxalic acid, and trim off the thick white ends. Wipe the stalks and chop into 2.5 cm/1 inch lengths. Put the fruit into a greased pan with a piece of orange peel and 2-3 tablespoons orange juice. Cook and purée as for apples.

Danish Apple Crunch

METRIC	IMPERIAL
1 kg Bramley apples	2 lb Bramley apples
sugar to taste	sugar to taste
100 g butter	4 oz butter
100 g breadcrumbs	4 oz breadcrumbs
100 g brown sugar	4 oz brown sugar
150-300 ml whipping cream, whipped	¼-½ pint whipping cream, whipped
1 bar chocolate flake	1 bar chocolate flake

Make a purée with the apples, sweeten to taste and cool. Heat the butter in a frying pan, stir in the breadcrumbs and fry lightly. Mix in the brown sugar and continue cooking until the breadcrumbs are crisp, but not hard. Remove the pan from the heat and stir the crumbs until cool. Put alternate layers of apple purée and fried crumbs in a glass bowl, finishing with crumbs. When cold, swirl over the whipped cream and decorate with spikes of chocolate flake. Chill until needed.

This popular pudding can be made with any other fruit purée. The apple version is called 'Peasant Girl with a Veil' in Denmark — the white cream veiling the homely apple purée.

Baked Fruits

Baked Apples

METRIC
4 Bramley apples
4 tablespoons mincemeat or
other stuffing (see below)
50 g butter
2-3 tablespoons brown sugar
75 ml cider or water

IMPERIAL
4 Bramley apples
4 tablespoons mincemeat or
other stuffing (see below)
2 oz butter
2-3 tablespoons brown sugar
3 fl oz cider or water

Step 1 Preheat the oven to 180 °C, 350 °F or gas mark 4. Push a corer through the centre of the apples, opening the hole to 3 cm/1½ inches. With the point of a sharp knife, slit the skin all round the middle or downwards in 6 segments. This prevents the apples bursting when they fluff up during cooking.

Step 2 Place the apples in a well-buttered ovenproof dish. Fill the centres with mincemeat or other stuffing such as chopped walnuts and cherries, ground almonds and honey, or just demerara or soft brown sugar.

Step 3 Top each apple with a knob of butter and sprinkle with brown sugar. Pour in sufficient cider or water to cover the base of the dish and place a piece of buttered paper on top of the apples.

Step 4 Bake in the oven for 30 minutes or longer according to size. Insert a skewer to test if they are tender; do not overcook. Serve hot or cold with pouring cream, custard or vanilla ice cream.

Pears in Red Wine

Unripe pears can be used for this dish, they will just take a longer time cooking. The rounded Comice or William pears are a good shape as they stand up better than the long Conference pears. Cider may be used instead of the wine and water.

METRIC	IMPERIAL
4 even-sized pears	4 even-sized pears
150 ml red wine	1/4 pint red wine
100 g caster sugar	4 oz caster sugar
approx. 300 ml water	approx. 1/2 pint water
1 long sliver lemon rind	1 long sliver lemon rind

Choose a deep flameproof casserole just large enough to take the pears standing up. Put in the wine, sugar, 150 ml/1/4 pint of the water and the lemon rind. Bring to the boil on top of the stove and simmer until syrupy. Peel the pears, leave on the stalks and level off the base. Stand the pears in the casserole and pour over the wine syrup. Add sufficient water just to cover the pears. Put on the lid and cook in a preheated oven at 160 °C, 325 °F or gas mark 3 for 1½ hours or until just tender; test with a skewer.

Chill thoroughly and serve with cream.

Baked Stuffed Peaches

METRIC	IMPERIAL
4 large peaches	4 large peaches
2 tablespoons rum or brandy	2 tablespoons rum or brandy
STUFFING	STUFFING
25 g caster sugar	1 oz caster sugar
50 g unsalted butter	2 oz unsalted butter
50 g ratafia biscuits	2 oz ratafia biscuits
1 egg yolk, beaten	1 egg yolk, beaten

To make the stuffing, cream the sugar and 25 g/1 oz of the butter together in a bowl. Crush the ratafia biscuits between two sheets of greaseproof paper, using a rolling pin, and work them into the creamed mixture. Bind with the egg yolk.

Plunge the peaches into boiling water for 2 to 3 minutes, then peel off the skin. Slit the peaches round the natural crease, and remove the stones. Grease a shallow ovenproof dish with the rest of the butter and put in the peach halves cut side up. Divide the stuffing into eight and fill the peach halves, doming the stuffing neatly. Cover the peaches with buttered greaseproof paper or foil and bake in a preheated oven at 180 °C, 350 °F or gas mark 4 for 20 minutes or until just cooked. Heat the rum or brandy in a small pan, set light to it and pour it flaming over the peaches. Serve immediately with whipped or clotted cream.

Meringues

Meringue is made with stiffly whisked egg white blended with sugar and it is essential that the egg is carefully separated (p. 151) and that the bowl and whisk are perfectly clean and dry. Even a drop of egg yolk, grease or water will prevent the white from whisking stiffly. For a small amount, a balloon whisk can be used, but a rotary whisk is quicker for larger quantities. When using an electric mixer, special care is needed to obtain exactly the right consistency for piping.

To make a meringue topping for a pudding or tart, 25 g/1 oz sugar to each egg white will be sufficient. This will give a crisp, golden surface when cooked for 30 minutes in a moderate oven, but it will be soft underneath. To make meringue shells or flan cases, which must be crisp all through, you need 50 g/2 oz sugar to each egg white and the meringue must be baked very slowly for 1 to 2 hours according to size. Unfilled shells can be stored for several days in an airtight tin, or frozen. Once filled, the meringue will soon soften.

Peach Meringue Flan

METRIC	IMPERIAL
2 egg whites	*2 egg whites*
100 g caster sugar	*4 oz caster sugar*
150 ml double cream	*¼ pint double cream*
½ kg fresh or canned peaches, sliced	*1 lb fresh or canned peaches, sliced*
chopped pistachio nuts to garnish	*chopped pistachio nuts to garnish*

Step 1 Line a baking tray with non-stick parchment or greaseproof paper. Draw on it in pencil 2 circles 18 cm/7 inch in diameter. Lightly oil the greaseproof paper. Preheat the oven to 140 °C, 275 °F or gas mark 1. Make meringue mixture with the egg whites and sugar (see facing page).

Step 2 Fit a large nozzle into a forcing bag and fill it with meringue mixture (p. 95 for detailed instructions). Pipe a ring of meringue round one circle just inside the pencil line. Pipe onto the parchment 8 to 12 baby rosettes with a base the same width as the meringue ring. Pipe the remaining mixture into the other circle and spread it out evenly into a flat disc.

Step 3 Bake the meringues in the preheated oven on a low shelf for 1 hour or until crisp when tapped. Remove the meringues from the oven. Lift off the rosettes with a knife. Turn the parchment upside down on the table and carefully peel it off the meringue ring and disc. If you try to prise the meringues off the parchment they are liable to splinter.

Shortly before serving, whip the cream and pipe a ring round the edge of the flat base. Place the meringue ring on top and press it down gently. Arrange the peach slices on the base in concentric circles. Pipe a little cream on the base of the rosettes and press them onto the ring. Decorate the flan with the remaining whipped cream and chopped pistachio nuts.

Meringues Chantilly

METRIC	IMPERIAL
2 egg whites	*2 egg whites*
50 g caster sugar	*2 oz caster sugar*
150 ml double cream	*¼ pint double cream*
extra caster sugar	*extra caster sugar*
vanilla essence to taste	*vanilla essence to taste*
chopped walnuts to garnish	*chopped walnuts to garnish*

Step 1 Preheat the oven to 120-140 °C, 250-275 °F or gas mark ½-1. Line a baking tray with non-stick parchment or grease and flour a baking sheet – bang it to spread the flour evenly. Using a rotary whisk and a large bowl, beat the egg whites until they are stiff and dry and hang on the whisk when shaken. Sift 2 tablespoons of the caster sugar over the whisked whites and beat again until stiff and shiny.

Step 2 Sift half the remaining sugar over the whites and, using a concave spatula or large cook's spoon, fold it in, scooping the mixture up from the bottom of the bowl and folding it over the top. Sift the rest of the sugar and fold it in, cutting down through the centre of the mixture. Work very quickly and lightly as too much folding will collapse the meringue.

Step 3 Take 2 large spoons and with one, scoop up a heaped spoonful of meringue. Then with the other, scoop it out of the spoon onto the baking sheet to form a shell shape. Neaten with a knife dipped in cold water. Dredge the shells with caster sugar. The shells can be piped with a large plain or rose nozzle if preferred. Bake the meringue in the oven on a low shelf for about 1 hour or until set and a delicate beige colour. Peel the parchment off meringues, or carefully lift them off with a sharp knife.

Step 4 Gently press the base of each shell in the centre to make a hollow and return the meringues upside down to the oven for another 30 minutes to dry out. Cool on a wire rack. Whip the cream until stiff. Sweeten with 1 teaspoon caster sugar and flavour with a few drops of vanilla essence. Sandwich the shells together in pairs with cream, which can be piped or spread with a teaspoon. Sprinkle with chopped walnuts. For a buffet, serve in paper cases.

Peach Meringue Flan; Meringues Chantilly

Caramel Puddings

Caramel is sugar boiled to such a high temperature (180°C, 350°F) that it acquires the colour and consistency of liquid toffee. There are two ways of making it – by dissolving the sugar in water before caramelizing it, as in the recipe for Crème caramel, or by dissolving it without any water as in Caramel queen of puddings. Liquid caramel is used to line moulds, flavour custards and sauces and to glaze various cakes and desserts.

Important points to watch

1. Remember boiling sugar is much hotter than boiling water and very sticky, so do not spill it and use thick oven gloves to handle moulds, tins etc.
2. Do not swirl the melting sugar or boiling syrup up the sides of the pan as the sugar will crystallize and fall back into the pan, granulating the syrup instead of caramelizing it.
3. Do not stir the syrup once it starts to boil or it will granulate. If it does, add more water, dissolve the syrup completely, then boil it up again.
4. To clean sticky pans and moulds, heat in boiling water, when the hard caramel will quickly and easily dissolve.

Caramel Queen of Puddings

METRIC	IMPERIAL
600 ml milk	1 pint milk
50 g sugar	2 oz sugar
300 ml fresh brown breadcrumbs	½ pint fresh brown breadcrumbs
2 egg yolks, beaten	2 egg yolks, beaten
3 tablespoons apricot jam	3 tablespoons apricot jam
MERINGUE	MERINGUE
2 egg whites	2 egg whites
50 g caster sugar	2 oz caster sugar
extra caster sugar for dredging	extra caster sugar for dredging

Heat the milk until it is nearly boiling. Spread the sugar over the base of a thick medium sized saucepan and heat it very gently until it has completely dissolved. Continue cooking until the syrup turns a good caramel colour. Remove from the heat and carefully pour in half the milk; the syrup will bubble up fiercely. Return to the heat and stir until the caramel is completely dissolved, then add the remaining milk. Pour the caramel milk over the breadcrumbs in a bowl and leave for 30 minutes for the bread to swell. Stir in the beaten egg yolks and pour into a buttered pie dish or large soufflé dish. Bake in a preheated oven at 180°C, 350°F or gas mark 4 for 30 minutes or until set. Remove the pudding from the oven and reduce the heat to 160°C, 325°F or gas mark 3. Warm the apricot jam and spread it over the pudding.

Make the meringue (p. 125). Spoon it on the top of the pudding, starting round the edge, then filling in the centre. Swirl the top and dredge with caster sugar. Return the pudding to the oven and continue cooking for 30 minutes or until the meringue is crisp and golden. Serve hot or cold.

Crème Caramel

METRIC	IMPERIAL
CARAMEL	CARAMEL
100 g caster sugar	*4 oz caster sugar*
4 tablespoons water	*4 tablespoons water*
CRÈME	CRÈME
375 ml milk	*¾ pint milk*
2 eggs	*2 eggs*
2 tablespoons sugar	*2 tablespoons sugar*
vanilla essence to flavour	*vanilla essence to flavour*

Step 1 Warm, but do not grease four 125 ml/¼ pint dariole moulds. Put the sugar and water for the caramel in a small thick pan and stir carefully over gentle heat until the sugar is completely dissolved. Do not swirl it up the sides of the pan – use a wet pastry brush to remove any splashes on sides of the pan.

Step 2 Remove the spoon from the pan, raise heat and boil *without stirring* until a golden caramel colour. To stop the caramel overbrowning, quickly dip the base of the pan in cold water. When the caramel is the right colour hold a mould in one hand, wearing oven gloves and pour in the caramel to about 2 cm/¾ inch deep.

Step 3 With the other gloved hand, rotate the mould so the caramel coats it evenly. Pour in a little more if needed.

Step 4 Preheat oven to 190°C, 375°F or gas mark 5. Heat the milk in a pan until a rim of bubbles appear round the edge. Beat eggs and sugar together, stir in milk. Add a few drops of vanilla essence.

Step 5 Pour custard into moulds. Put in a *bain marie* (3½ cm/1½ inch water in a roasting pan). Cover with greased paper or foil, cook in centre of oven for 45 minutes or until set. Test by gently shaking moulds; the centre should be as firm as jelly.

Step 6 Chill the crèmes thoroughly. To unmould, place individual serving bowls over the top of the crèmes, hold the mould and bowl firmly and invert. Give a slight shake and carefully lift off the mould. The caramel will run down the crèmes as a golden sauce. Serve with cream.
Note: Crème caramel may be cooked in a 600 ml/1 pint mould. It will require 1 hour or longer to cook and is best chilled overnight.

Steamed Puddings

There are many types of steamed puddings, from rich and substantial suet puddings to light and delicate sponges. They can be steamed on top of the stove or in a slow oven, where they need little attention. Steamed puddings seldom suffer from overcooking, which is very convenient for late-comers to the table.

To cover steamed puddings

A steamed pudding must be covered before cooking to prevent the steam which condenses on the saucepan lid from falling back onto the pudding and making it soggy.

For Christmas and suet puddings

Lay a small piece of buttered paper on top of the pudding. Cover with a cotton square 3 times wider than the top of the pudding basin. Fold in a pleat 2½ cm/1 inch deep across the centre. Twist a piece of string twice round the basin below the rim and tie it securely. Open the pleat to allow the pudding to rise during cooking.

Knot opposite corners of the square together above the pudding – this makes a convenient handle to lift the pudding in and out of the saucepan.

For sponge puddings

Select a pudding basin or aluminium mould large enough to allow the pudding to rise well during cooking. Cover with a square of buttered kitchen foil and tie it down securely.

For steaming methods 1 & 2

Three-quarters fill a plastic pudding basin which has a snap on lid. Butter the inside of the lid and fit it on securely. Steam the pudding by method 1 or 2, *NEVER* in a pressure cooker as the heat is too intense for plastic.

To steam puddings

Method 1

Heat sufficient boiling water in a saucepan to come half-way up the pudding basin. Place the covered pudding in a pan-converter and, using the hooks, lift it into the pan and detach the hooks.

OR if no pan-converter is available, make a sling with a broad strip of doubled kitchen foil, long enough to afford a firm grip when lifting the pudding in and out of the saucepan.
Put on the saucepan lid and make sure the water is kept simmering, but does not boil up over the pudding. Top up with boiling water from the kettle as the water in the pan evaporates. Pour it in carefully so that it does not run over the top of the pudding.

Method 2

Put the covered pudding in a steamer and place over a saucepan half-filled with simmering water. Put on lid and make sure the water does not boil away under the steamer, as the pudding will take from 30 minutes longer to cook than when half immersed in boiling water.

Method 3

Ovensteaming eliminates the necessity for topping up as there is much less evaporation. Place the covered pudding in a deep casserole with boiling water to come half-way up the basin. Cover closely and cook in the oven at 160°C, 325°F or gas mark 3.

Method 4

Steam the pudding in a pressure cooker. This is the quickest method, but be sure to follow the manufacturer's instructions precisely.

College Pudding

METRIC	IMPERIAL
50 g plain flour	2 oz plain flour
1 teaspoon baking powder	1 teaspoon baking powder
½ teaspoon mixed spice	½ teaspoon mixed spice
pinch of salt	pinch of salt
50 g shredded suet	2 oz shredded suet
25 g white or brown sugar	1 oz white or brown sugar
75 g mixed currants, raisins and sultanas	3 oz mixed currants, raisins and sultanas
25 g chopped candied peel or glacé cherries	1 oz chopped candied peel or glacé cherries
50 g fresh breadcrumbs	2 oz fresh breadcrumbs
1 egg, beaten	1 egg, beaten
4-5 tablespoons milk	4-5 tablespoons milk

Prepare a steamer (see facing page) and butter a 900 ml/1½ pint pudding basin. Sift the flour, baking powder, spice and salt into a mixing bowl and mix in the suet, sugar, fruit and breadcrumbs. Stir in the egg and sufficient milk to produce a soft consistency which drops off the spoon in 5 seconds.

Turn the mixture into the pudding basin, which should be two-thirds full. Cover with greased foil or a snap-on lid. Steam for 2 to 2½ hours (see facing page). When cooked, allow the pudding to shrink slightly then cover the basin with a hot serving plate, hold it firmly and invert. Carefully lift off the basin. Serve the pudding hot with Custard (p. 30) or Brandy butter (p. 31) if liked.

Variations

Spotted Dick or Currant Duff

Make as for College pudding, using 100 g/4 oz currants instead of mixed fruit. Serve with Custard (p.30) if liked.

Date or Fig Pudding

Use 100 g/4 oz chopped dates or figs instead of dried fruit and add the grated rind of ½ lemon. Delicious served with Orange custard (p. 30).

Marmalade Pudding

Use ½ teaspoon bicarbonate of soda instead of baking powder and stir in 2 tablespoons marmalade instead of fruit. Serve with marmalade, heated and thinned with a little water.

College Pudding; Marmalade Pudding

Steamed Sponge Puddings

These are much lighter than the puddings made with suet and breadcrumbs, as the fat is not rubbed in, but creamed with the sugar as for a sponge cake mixture.

Points to remember

1. Do not use butter straight from the refrigerator; allow it to soften at room temperature, but do not let it melt as this will make the pudding heavy.
2. Beat the butter and sugar together until really pale in colour and fluffy. Beat it with a wooden spoon, or use an electric mixer at low speed. Do not let the mixer run too long as it will liquidize the mixture and make it heavy.
3. Beat in the eggs a spoonful at a time and beat well between additions. If the mixture starts to curdle, add a spoonful of the measured flour each time egg is added.
4. Fold in the flour quickly and lightly, using a concave spatula or a large cook's spoon. An electric mixer produces a much closer texture.

Black Cherry Castle Puddings

METRIC	IMPERIAL
100 g butter or margarine	4 oz butter or margarine
100 g caster sugar	4 oz caster sugar
2 eggs, beaten	2 eggs, beaten
100 g plain flour	4 oz plain flour
2 teaspoons baking powder	2 teaspoons baking powder
¼ teaspoon vanilla essence	¼ teaspoon vanilla essence
1-2 tablespoons warm water	1-2 tablespoons warm water
3 tablespoons black cherry jam	3 tablespoons black cherry jam

Cream the butter and sugar and make up the sponge mixture as for Golden orange sponge (see facing page), flavouring it with vanilla instead of orange.

Grease four 150 ml/¼ pint dariole moulds or six small castle pudding tins. Put a good teaspoon of cherry jam in the bottom of each one. Two-thirds fill the moulds with sponge mixture and stand them in a baking tin with boiling water to come half-way up the moulds. Cover with a sheet of buttered greaseproof paper or foil. Bake in the centre of a preheated oven at 180°C, 350°F or gas mark 4 for 50 minutes, or until set. Test with a skewer, which should come out clean. Allow the puddings to shrink slightly and if necessary trim off the top level with the rim of the moulds. Turn out onto a hot serving platter.

Golden Orange Sponge

METRIC	IMPERIAL
1 orange	1 orange
2-3 tablespoons golden syrup	2-3 tablespoons golden syrup
SPONGE MIXTURE	**SPONGE MIXTURE**
100 g butter or margarine	4 oz butter or margarine
100 g caster sugar	4 oz caster sugar
2 eggs, beaten	2 eggs, beaten
100 g plain flour	4 oz plain flour
2 teaspoons baking powder	2 teaspoons baking powder
1-2 tablespoons warm water	1-2 tablespoons warm water

Step 1 Prepare a steamer and grease a 900 ml/1½ pint pudding basin. Finely grate the rind off the orange. Remove peel and pith and cut out segments as for fruit salad (p. 119), catching juice in a plate. Reserve juice. Spread syrup over bottom of basin and arrange orange segments on it to resemble a daisy.

Black Cherry Castle Puddings; Golden Orange Sponge

Spoon the mixture into the bowl on top of the orange segments. Cover and steam (p. 128) for 1½ hours or until set. Test with a skewer, which should come out clean. Remove the pudding basin from the pan, allow the pudding to shrink slightly and unmould it on to a hot platter. Serve with Orange custard (p. 30) if liked.

Step 2 Cream the butter and sugar together in a bowl until very light and fluffy.

Step 3 Gradually beat in the eggs, 1 tablespoon at a time, and beat well between each addition to avoid curdling. Should the mixture start to separate, add 1 tablespoon of flour with each addition of egg.

Step 4 Sift the flour and baking powder together and fold it into the mixture quickly and lightly, using a concave spatula or a long cook's spoon (see folding, p. 36). Add the reserved orange juice and enough water to give a soft dropping consistency; it should fall off the spoon in 5 seconds.

English Fruit Pies

The traditional English fruit pie is made in a deep pie dish with fresh fruit in season, covered with plain shortcrust pastry. It is usually served hot with cream or with custard, but it can also be eaten cold.

Blackberry and Pear Pie

METRIC	IMPERIAL
225 g blackberries	*8 oz blackberries*
½ kg cooking pears	*1 lb cooking pears*
4-5 tablespoons sugar	*4-5 tablespoons sugar*
225 g Plain shortcrust pastry (p. 82)	*8 oz Plain shortcrust pastry (p. 82)*
caster sugar for dredging	*caster sugar for dredging*

Pick over the blackberries, removing any hulls, and wash if necessary. Quarter the pears, then peel, core and slice them. Fill a deep 900 ml/1½ pint pie dish with the fruit, piling the layers of sliced pears and blackberries into a dome. Sprinkle each layer with sugar. Add 2 tablespoons water.

On a floured board, roll out the pastry 5 mm/¼ inch thick to the same shape as the top of the pie dish but a little larger. Damp the lip of the dish. Cut off and press on strips of pastry, damp the strips and cover with the remaining pastry (for detailed pictures see p. 90, and follow steps 2, 3 and 4). Flute the edge (step 3, opposite) if you wish, but to distinguish a fruit from a meat pie, the edge should really be crimped with the tines of a fork. With the left thumb, press the knocked back pastry edge down firmly and holding the fork vertically, press the tines of the fork against the outer edge of the pastry, marking it neatly in grooves (below).

It is not correct to decorate the pie with pastry leaves as for steak pie; instead, prick through the pastry with the fork in a simple design.

Bake in a preheated oven at 200 °C, 400 °F or gas mark 6 for 30-40 minutes, until the fruit is cooked and the pastry is crisp and golden. Remove the pie from oven, place it on serving dish and dredge with caster sugar. Serve with clotted or pouring cream or custard.

Spiced Apple Pie; Blackberry and Pear Pie

Variations

Use ¾ kg/1½ lb sliced apples and 1 teaspoon ground cinnamon or cloves mixed with brown sugar.

Use 1 kg/2 lb prepared rhubarb (p. 121) with 1 teaspoon ground ginger mixed with sugar.

Use 1 kg/2 lb plums, apricots or greengages, halved and stoned (p. 119) or gooseberries, topped and tailed, with white or brown sugar.

Double Crust Fruit Pies

These pies are made in a shallow round pie dish with the fruit sandwiched between two layers of pastry. You can use plain or sweet shortcrust. Be sure to chill the sweet pastry, otherwise the dough will be tricky to roll out and handle.

Spiced Apple Pie

METRIC
225 g Shortcrust pastry,
  plain or rich (p. 82, 84)
75 g white or brown sugar
1 tablespoon flour
¼ teaspoon grated nutmeg
¼ teaspoon ground
  cinnamon
finely grated rind and juice
  of 1 orange
finely grated rind of 1 lemon
¾ kg cooking apples, sliced
50 g sultanas
1 tablespoon lemon juice
40 g butter, melted
TO GLAZE
milk or beaten egg white
granulated sugar

IMPERIAL
8 oz Shortctust pastry, plain
  or rich (p. 82, 84)
3 oz white or brown sugar
1 tablespoon flour
¼ teaspoon grated nutmeg
¼ teaspoon ground
  cinnamon
finely grated rind and juice
  of 1 orange
finely grated rind of 1 lemon
1½ lb cooking apples, sliced
2 oz sultanas
1 tablespoon lemon juice
1½ oz butter, melted
TO GLAZE
milk or beaten egg white
granulated sugar

Step 1 Preheat the oven to 200 °C, 400 °F or gas mark 6. Grease the base of a 20 cm/8 inch round shallow pie dish. Divide the pastry in half and roll out one half thinly into a round. Damp the lip of the pie dish, line it with the pastry and prick all over the base with a fork. Mix together the sugar, flour and spices and rub a little over the pastry base. Add grated orange and lemon rind to remainder. Arrange the sliced apples in the dish, sprinkle each layer with sultanas, sugar mixture, fruit juice and melted butter.

Step 2 Roll out the other piece of pastry into a round about 5 cm/2 inches larger all round than the top of the pie dish. Damp the edge of the bottom pastry. Lift the other piece on the rolling pin and unroll it across the top of the pie (step 2, p. 90). Press the two edges firmly together and with a sharp knife trim off the surplus pastry and knock it back (step 4, p. 91).

Step 3 To flute the edge: with the left forefinger, press the pastry edge down and slightly off the rim of the dish and with the thumb and forefinger of the other hand press the pastry into a peak. Repeat evenly round the edge of the pie. Make a few slits in the top of the pie to allow the steam to escape during cooking.

Bake in the oven for 20 minutes or until the pastry is well risen and turning golden. Lower the heat to 190 °C, 375 °F or gas mark 5 and cook for another 25 minutes, or until the filling is cooked. Serve hot with cream or custard.

Flans (Open Tarts)

For flans with sweet fillings it is better to use sweet shortcrust rather than plain, and leave it to cool and relax well before rolling it out.

Fresh Strawberry Flan

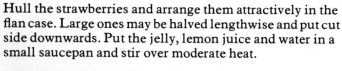

METRIC	IMPERIAL
1 18-20 cm Sweet shortcrust flan case, baked blind (p. 83)	*1 7-8 inch Sweet shortcrust flan case, baked blind (p. 83)*
375-450 g fresh strawberries	*12-16 oz fresh strawberries*
4 tablespoons redcurrant jelly	*4 tablespoons redcurrant jelly*
1 tablespoon lemon juice	*1 tablespoon lemon juice*
2 tablespoons water	*2 tablespoons water*

Hull the strawberries and arrange them attractively in the flan case. Large ones may be halved lengthwise and put cut side downwards. Put the jelly, lemon juice and water in a small saucepan and stir over moderate heat.

When the jelly is completely dissolved, boil briskly until the glaze hangs on the wooden spoon for a few seconds before it drops off. If the glaze is too thin it will not set, but if overcooked it will set into a soft toffee-like consistency.

Flow most of the glaze carefully all over the fruit using the side of a large metal spoon; do not trickle it. To give an elegant finish, brush the top edge of the flan with the remaining glaze.

When cold, decorate the flan with piped cream or serve it in a separate bowl.

Variations

Fill the flan with fresh raspberries or loganberries, or stoned cherries and coat with redcurrant jelly.

Fill with the halved and stoned apricots, plums or greengages, or sliced peaches or fresh pineapple. Use 6 tablespoons sieved apricot jam instead of redcurrant jelly to make the glaze.

Fill with canned fruit, coat with redcurrant jelly glaze if using red fruit, or apricot glaze if fruit is yellow, or green and red mixed.

Lemon Meringue Pie

This popular dessert can be made with plain or sweet shortcrust. Do not over-sweeten as the sharpness of the filling should be a contrast to the sweet meringue topping.

METRIC	IMPERIAL
1 18-20 cm plain or sweet Shortcrust flan case, baked blind (p. 82)	*1 7-8 inch plain or sweet Shortcrust flan case, baked blind (p. 82)*
1 large or 2 small lemons	*1 large or 2 small lemons*
2 tablespoons cornflour	*2 tablespoons cornflour*
2 egg yolks, beaten	*2 egg yolks, beaten*
sugar to taste	*sugar to taste*
MERINGUE TOPPING	MERINGUE TOPPING
2 egg whites	*2 egg whites*
50 g caster sugar	*2 oz caster sugar*
glacé cherries and angelica leaves to decorate	*glacé cherries and angelica leaves to decorate*
extra caster sugar for dredging	*extra caster sugar for dredging*

Fresh Strawberry Flan; Lemon Meringue Pie

Grate the rind finely off the lemons. Squeeze out the juice, measure it and make it up to 225 ml/8 fl oz with water. In a small saucepan blend the cornflour to a thin paste with a little of the lemon liquid. Gradually stir in the rest of the liquid and the zest, bring to the simmer and cook for 3 to 4 minutes, stirring steadily. Blend 2 tablespoons of the mixture into the egg yolks and stir this back into the saucepan. Sweeten to taste.

Cool the filling, pour it into the flan case and smooth over. Preheat the oven to 160 °C, 325 °F or gas mark 3. Whisk the egg whites until very stiff and dry. Sift and fold in the sugar quickly and lightly (p. 125). Spoon the meringue round the edge of the filling and then fill in the centre.

Be sure that the meringue is well sealed to the pastry edge or the steam from any uncovered filling will make the meringue 'weep'.

Swirl the top of the meringue with a spatula or palette knife. Decorate with glacé cherries and angelica leaves. Dredge lightly with caster sugar and bake in the centre of the oven for 30 minutes or until crisp and golden.

Baking Scones and Cakes

The basic ingredients for making scones and cakes consist of flour and fat in varying proportions, with a raising agent such as baking powder, yeast or eggs, and for sweet mixtures white or brown sugar, treacle or honey.

The fat is rubbed in (see Plain shortcrust pastry p. 82) when making plain scones and cakes, but creamed with the sugar for richer mixtures or melted with the sweetener for gingerbread.

Some light sponges are fatless, and are made by whisking the sugar with the eggs and just folding in the flour.

Scones

Scones can be mixed and baked in 20 minutes and are very handy if you run out of bread. They can be served hot, split and spread with butter, or cooled and spread with jam or honey, or filled with clotted cream and strawberry jam like Devonshire splits. They can be baked in a very hot oven or on a girdle. Self-raising flour does not give such a good rise as baking powder or bicarbonate of soda with cream of tartar and buttermilk.

Variations

Sultana Scones

Add 50 g/2 oz sultanas and 1-2 tablespoons caster sugar to the dry ingredients and mix with 1 beaten egg and 75 ml/3 fl oz water. Glaze with milk.

Cheese Scones

Add 75-100 g/3-4 oz grated mature cheese to the dry ingredients with 1 teaspoon dry mustard. Mix the dough with 150 ml/¼ pint milk.

Oven Scones

METRIC	IMPERIAL
25-50 g butter or margarine	*1-2 oz butter or margarine*
225 g plain flour	*8 oz plain flour*
½ teaspoon salt	*½ teaspoon salt*
4 teaspoons baking powder	*4 teaspoons baking powder*
approx. 150 ml milk	*approx. ¼ pint milk*
milk or flour to finish	*milk or flour to finish*

Step 1 Preheat the oven to 230 °C, 450 °F or gas mark 8 and heat a baking sheet. Sift the flour, salt and baking powder into a mixing bowl. Chop up the fat and rub it into the flour (step 1, Plain shortcrust pastry, p. 82).

Step 2 Make a well in the centre and pour in most of the liquid. Mix to a soft spongy dough, adding more liquid as needed. Turn on to a well floured board and quickly knead out any cracks.

Step 3 Pat out dough, or roll lightly, until ½ cm/¾ inch thick. Cut into rounds with floured scone cutter 6 cm/2½ inches wide put onto warmed baking sheet. Reshape remaining dough into a ball, flatten slightly, cut into quarters. Put triangles on baking sheet.

Step 4 Brush the scones with milk for a glossy top, or dust with flour for a soft crust. Bake near the top of the oven for 7 to 10 minutes until the scones are well risen and golden brown. Remove from the oven and wrap in a tea cloth if to be served hot, or cool on a wire tray.

Picnic Cake (Quick Fruit Cake)

METRIC	IMPERIAL
225 g plain flour	8 oz plain flour
1 teaspoon baking powder	1 teaspoon baking powder
1 teaspoon mixed spice	1 teaspoon mixed spice
grated rind of ½ lemon or	grated rind of ½ lemon or
grated rind of 1 orange	grated rind of 1 orange
100 g butter or margarine	4 oz butter or margarine
100 g caster sugar	4 oz caster sugar
50 g sultanas	2 oz sultanas
50 g currants, cleaned	2 oz currants, cleaned
50 g seedless raisins	2 oz seedless raisins
2 eggs, beaten	2 eggs, beaten
4 glacé cherries	4 glacé cherries
4 walnut halves	4 walnut halves
extra sugar for sprinkling	extra sugar for sprinkling

Preheat the oven to 190 °C, 375 °F or gas mark 5.

Sift the flour, baking powder and spice into a mixing bowl and add the grated rind. Chop up the fat and rub it in lightly to give breadcrumb consistency. Add the sugar, sultanas, currants and raisins and mix well. Stir in the beaten eggs and, if necessary, add a little water to give a soft dropping consistency – the mixture should drop off the spoon in 5 seconds.

Put the mixture into a greased 15 cm/6 inch round cake tin. Arrange the glacé cherries and walnut halves on top. Sprinkle with a little sugar.

Bake in the oven for 15 minutes then reduce the heat to 180 °C, 350 °F or gas mark 4 and bake for a further 1¼ hours or until the cake is done, when a skewer inserted in the centre should come out clean. Allow the cake to shrink a little in the tin, then turn it out onto a wire tray to cool.

Rock Buns

Make up the Picnic cake mixture into a fairly stiff dough – if too soft the buns will spread instead of being rocky. Using 2 forks, put the mixture into small heaps on a greased baking tin. Bake in a preheated oven at 220 °C, 425 °F or gas mark 7 for about 15 minutes or until set and golden brown.

Oven Scones; Picnic Cake (Quick Fruit Cake); Rock Buns

Creamed Cakes

Victoria Sandwich

This rich sponge mixture, with the basis of butter and sugar creamed together, is the foundation of a variety of cakes and puddings. The traditional recipe tells the cook to use 'the weight of 3 eggs in sugar and flour', and you may still prefer to put your eggs on the scales instead of weights.

See p. 131 for special points to remember when making a creamed sponge mixture.

See p. 131

METRIC	IMPERIAL
150 g butter or margarine	6 oz butter or margarine
150 g caster sugar	6 oz caster sugar
3 eggs, beaten	3 eggs, beaten
150 g plain flour	6 oz plain flour
2 teaspoons baking powder	2 teaspoons baking powder
1-2 tablespoons water	1-2 tablespoons water
extra caster sugar for dredging	extra caster sugar for dredging

Step 1 Grease two 18 cm/7 inch sandwich tins. If the tins do not have a lever to release the sponge, line the base of each with a round of buttered greaseproof paper. Preheat the oven to 190 °C, 375 °F or gas mark 5.

Cream the butter and sugar together until light and fluffy, then gradually beat in the eggs a spoonful at a time. Sift the flour and baking powder together and fold it into the mixture. Add a little water to give a soft dropping consistency – it should drop off the spoon in 5 seconds.

Victoria Sandwich; Dundee Cake

Step 2 Divide the mixture between the two tins, and smooth the top. Bake both cakes side by side in the oven for 20 minutes or until they are well risen and golden. When cooked, they will be springy to the touch and beginning to shrink away from the side of the tin. Allow the cakes to shrink slightly, then turn them out upside down on a wire tray to cool.

Step 3 When cool, remove the cakes from the tray, spread one with jam, place the other on top and dredge with caster sugar.

Dundee Cake

This popular fruit cake is a rich mixture, made by the creaming method (p. 131), which keeps well and indeed should be allowed to mature for a month before it is cut.

METRIC	IMPERIAL
100 g sultanas	4 oz sultanas
100 g seedless raisins	4 oz seedless raisins
100 g currants	4 oz currants
50 g chopped mixed peel	2 oz chopped mixed peel
50 g halved glacé cherries	2 oz halved glacé cherries
50 g blanched almonds	2 oz blanched almonds
275 g plain flour	10 oz plain flour
1 teaspoon mixed spice	1 teaspoon mixed spice
225 g butter or margarine	8 oz butter or margarine
225 g soft brown sugar	8 oz soft brown sugar
grated rind of 1 lemon	grated rind of 1 lemon
4 eggs, beaten	4 eggs, beaten
little milk to finish	little milk to finish

Line a 20 cm/8 inch round cake tin (p. 151).

Pick over the fruit, clean the currants, if necessary, by rubbing them in flour in a wire sieve. Set aside some almonds for decoration and cut the remainder into long slivers. Sieve the flour and spice into a mixing bowl and mix in the fruit and nuts.

Cream the fat and sugar together with the grated lemon rind until light and fluffy. Beat in the eggs a spoonful at a time, beating well between additions. Fold in the flour, fruit and nuts. The mixture should drop off the spoon in 5 seconds, add a spoonful of water if needed.

Spoon the cake mixture into the lined tin, spreading it evenly. Now make a large hollow in the centre. This will fill in during the first hour of baking and the cake will rise evenly instead of in a dome. Split the remaining almonds, toss them in a saucer of milk and arrange them on top of the cake.

Bake in the centre of a preheated oven at 160 °C, 325 °F or gas mark 3 for 2 to 3 hours. If the top is browning too quickly, cover it with brown paper. Test by inserting a skewer, not a cold knife, into the centre of the cake; it will come out clean when the cake is cooked.

When cooked, remove the cake from the oven and allow it to cool in the tin. If the top has cracked, turn the cake upside down on a cooling tray and the weight will close any cracks. When cool, lift off the tin and peel off the paper. When quite cold, put the cake in an airtight tin or seal it in a plastic bag and store for four weeks before cutting.

Whisked Sponges

This fatless sponge is the lightest of the sponge mixtures and is conveniently quick to make, especially with an electric mixer – if you do not have one use a rotary or balloon whisk. If you use an electric mixer for the eggs and sugar, still fold in the flour with a concave spatula or large metal spoon, for a really light texture.

This sponge does not need any raising agent, as the eggs and vigorous whisking produces a very light texture. A whisked sponge should be eaten fresh as it tends to dry out when stored, unless it is frozen. A butter cream filling and topping adds richness to cakes; sponge puddings may be soaked with fruit juice, sherry or liqueur.

Basic Whisked Sponge

METRIC	IMPERIAL
3 eggs	*3 eggs*
¼ teaspoon vanilla essence	*¼ teaspoon vanilla essence*
75 g caster sugar	*3 oz caster sugar*
75 g plain flour	*3 oz plain flour*
FILLING AND TOPPING	FILLING AND TOPPING
250 g Chocolate butter cream (p. 142)	*9 oz Chocolate butter cream (p. 142)*
2 tablespoons finely chopped walnuts	*2 tablespoons finely chopped walnuts*
9 walnut halves	*9 walnut halves*
chopped pistachio nuts or angelica leaves to decorate	*chopped pistachio nuts or angelica leaves to decorate*

Step 1 Grease two 18 cm/7 inch sandwich tins and dust with a mixture of 1 teaspoon each of sugar and flour. Preheat the oven to 190 °C, 375 °F or gas mark 5.

Whisk the eggs, vanilla and sugar together until really pale; the mixture should fall off the whisk in ribbons which hold their shape on top of the mixture on the bowl for several seconds before sinking.

Step 2 Sift half the flour and fold it into the egg mixture quickly and lightly. Sift and fold in remaining flour. Pour the mixture into the sandwich tins, tilt them to spread it out evenly. Bang the tin on the table to settle mixture. Bake cakes on the same oven shelf for 20 minutes until well risen and golden and tops are springy to touch. Remove the cakes from the oven allow to shrink slightly before turning out on to a wire tray to cool.

Step 3 Take one-third of the chocolate butter cream and mix in the chopped walnuts. Sandwich the two sponges together with this filling. Spread the rest of the butter cream neatly over the top of the cake. Make a swirling pattern with a knife, or mark it into squares with the tines of a fork. Arrange the walnut halves on top and finish with lines or groups of chopped pistachio nuts or small angelica leaves.

Jam Swiss Roll; Basic Whisked Sponge

Jam Swiss Roll

METRIC
3 eggs
75 g caster sugar
½ teaspoon vanilla essence
75 g plain flour
1 tablespoon warm water
100 g warmed jam
extra caster sugar for
   dredging

IMPERIAL
3 eggs
3 oz caster sugar
½ teaspoon vanilla essence
3 oz plain flour
1 tablespoon warm water
4 oz warmed jam
extra caster sugar for
   dredging

Step 1 Line a 23 × 30 cm/9 × 12 inch Swiss roll tin with greaseproof paper or non-stick parchment. Cut a rectangle 5 cm/2 inches larger all round than the tin. Grease bottom of the tin to prevent paper slipping about. Lay paper in tin and, using the handle of a metal spoon, press paper into the angle all round base of the tin, making a firm crease. Using scissors, snip the paper from each corner down to corner of the tin. Brush with oil; this is not necessary with non-stick parchment.

Step 2 Preheat oven to 220 °C, 425 °F or gas mark 7. Make up sponge mixture, as on facing page. Pour into the tin and spread it evenly into corners with a spatula. Bake near top of oven for 8 to 10 minutes, until golden and springy to touch. Meanwhile wring out a clean teacloth in hot water. Spread it on the table, place a sheet of greaseproof paper on top and dredge lightly with sugar. This will facilitate the rolling up.

Step 3 When the sponge is ready – do not overcook it or it will be brittle to roll up – turn it upside down on the sugared paper. Carefully ease up the edges of the lining paper and peel it off. With a long knife trim off the crisp side edges of the sponge. Cut a shallow slit, parallel with the bottom edge and 1 cm/½ inch above it.

Step 4 Spread the warmed jam over the sponge. Turn the bottom edge up and tuck it in so the first roll is fairly tight. Then, using the paper, continue rolling more lightly and evenly into a neat roll with the joint underneath. Place the Swiss roll on a serving plate and dredge with a little more caster sugar.

Cake Fillings and Icings

Vanilla Butter Cream

METRIC
75 g butter
175 g icing sugar, sifted
¼ teaspoon vanilla essence
  or other flavouring
1-2 teaspoons warm water
Makes 250 g/9 oz

IMPERIAL
3 oz butter
6 oz icing sugar, sifted
¼ teaspoon vanilla essence
  or other flavouring
1-2 teaspoons warm water

Cream the butter until soft and gradually beat in the icing sugar. Add the flavouring essence and a little warm water if necessary to give a smooth pliable texture. This amount will cover the top and sides of an 18 cm/7 inch sponge sandwich or be sufficient for a filling and topping.

Variations

Chocolate Butter Cream
Replace 25 g/1 oz icing sugar with 25 g/1 oz cocoa or chocolate powder. Flavour to taste with vanilla essence.

Orange and Lemon Butter Cream
Cream the butter and sugar with the finely grated rind of ½ lemon or 1 small orange. Add the strained juice a little at a time or the butter cream will curdle.

Coffee Butter Cream
Add 2 teaspoons instant coffee powder to the icing sugar. Cream with the butter, add a little water if necessary.

Mocha Butter Cream
Add 1 teaspoon instant coffee powder and 1 tablespoon cocoa or chocolate powder to the icing sugar. Cream with the butter, add a little water.

Walnut Butter Cream
Add 2 tablespoons finely chopped walnuts to the finished vanilla, chocolate, coffee or mocha butter cream.

Rich Gingerbread; Party Gingerbread

Glacé Icing

METRIC
100 g icing sugar
water to mix
vanilla essence

IMPERIAL
4 oz icing sugar
water to mix
vanilla essence

Sift the icing sugar into a small bowl. Gradually stir in the water, a spoonful at a time, to give a spreading consistency. Add a few drops of vanilla essence. Use the icing at once as it sets quickly. This quantity is sufficient to coat the top of an 18 cm/7 inch cake.

Variations

Lemon or Orange Glacé Icing
Use strained lemon or orange juice instead of water to mix and add a few drops of yellow or orange colouring if desired.

Coffee Glacé Icing
Sift 2 teaspoons instant coffee powder with the icing sugar.

Gingerbread

Gingerbreads vary in richness, but the traditional dark sticky kind is made with black treacle. This is melted with the butter and beaten into the dry ingredients to make a thick batter, which is then slowly baked. Gingerbread can be eaten hot or cold; it keeps and matures well when cooled and stored.

Rich Gingerbread

METRIC	IMPERIAL
100 g butter or margarine	*4 oz butter or margarine*
175 g black treacle	*6 oz black treacle*
50 g golden syrup	*2 oz golden syrup*
50 g soft brown sugar	*2 oz soft brown sugar*
150 ml milk	*¼ pint milk*
2 eggs, beaten	*2 eggs, beaten*
225 g plain flour	*8 oz plain flour*
2 teaspoons mixed spice	*2 teaspoons mixed spice*
2 teaspoons ground ginger	*2 teaspoons ground ginger*
1 teaspoon bicarbonate of soda	*1 teaspoon bicarbonate of soda*
50 g sultanas or seedless raisins (optional)	*2 oz sultanas or seedless raisins (optional)*
50 g chopped stem ginger (optional)	*2 oz chopped stem ginger (optional)*

Grease a 1 kg/2 lb loaf tin. Line the bottom with a strip of non-stick parchment or greaseproof paper. Preheat the oven to 150 °C, 300 °F or gas mark 2. Weigh a mug and measure into it the required weight of treacle.

Step 1 Put the fat, treacle, golden syrup and sugar in a saucepan and heat it gradually until melted. With a wooden spoon, stir in the milk, then cool slightly and stir in the beaten eggs.

Step 2 Sift together into a bowl the flour, spice, ginger and bicarbonate of soda. Make a well in the centre of the dry ingredients, stir in the egg mixture and beat vigorously until smooth. Sprinkle over the dried fruit and fold it in. Repeat with the chopped ginger, if used.

Step 3 Pour the mixture into the prepared tin. Bake in the centre of the oven for 1½ to 2 hours. Test with a skewer, which will come out clean when the gingerbread is cooked. Allow the gingerbread to shrink slightly in the tin before turning it out onto a wire tray.

For *Party Gingerbread*: When cold, spread the top of the gingerbread with 100 g/4 oz white Lemon flavoured glacé icing (see facing page) and decorate with pieces of crystallized (not stem) ginger.

Girdle Cooking

This is a popular way of baking in the North Country, Scotland and in Wales, where the girdle is called a bakestone. In America it is called a griddle. It is a heavy iron plate, usually with a hooped handle that folds down for easy storage. A really heavy-based frying pan can be used if it is absolutely flat. Some gas and electric stoves incorporate a griddle plate.

To prepare the girdle, rub it with salt while heating it slowly, then clean it off with kitchen paper and grease it. If the girdle is too hot the scones will burn underneath before being cooked through. To test the temperature, sprinkle the girdle with a little flour, which should turn light brown in 3 minutes.

Girdle Scones

Follow the recipe for Oven scones (p. 136), replacing the baking powder with 1 teaspoon bicarbonate of soda and 2 teaspoons cream of tartar and adding 2 tablespoons caster sugar. Divide the dough in half and roll it into 2 rounds 1 cm/½ inch thick. Cut each round into 6 triangles. Cook on the greased girdle for 5 minutes until well risen and golden underneath, then turn and cook for a further 10 minutes or until nicely browned and cooked through.

Irish Potato Cakes; Ten-Minute Pancakes

Ten-Minute Pancakes

METRIC	IMPERIAL
100 g plain flour	*4 oz plain flour*
2 teaspoons baking powder	*2 teaspoons baking powder*
1 tablespoon caster sugar	*1 tablespoon caster sugar*
1 egg, separated	*1 egg, separated*
150 ml milk	*¼ pint milk*
1 tablespoon melted butter	*1 tablespoon melted butter*
50 g sultanas or currants or	*2 oz sultanas or currants or*
seedless raisins	*seedless raisins*

Sift the flour, baking powder and caster sugar into a mixing bowl. Make a well in the centre and quickly stir in the egg yolk, milk and melted butter; do not beat it. Whisk the egg white until stiff, and fold it in quickly and lightly. Sprinkle on the dried fruit and fold it in. Heat and lightly grease the girdle. It is the right temperature when a drop of water splutters on the surface.

Drop the batter off the point of a large metal spoon, allowing room for spreading.

Cook for 2-3 minutes until the bubbles burst through the batter, turn with a palette knife and cook until golden. When cooked, wrap the pancakes in a clean cloth to keep them warm and soft. Serve with butter, honey or jam.

Irish Potato Cakes

METRIC
½ kg floury potatoes
50 g butter
salt and pepper to taste
approx. 100 g plain flour
butter for filling

IMPERIAL
1 lb floury potatoes
2 oz butter
salt and pepper to taste
approx. 4 oz plain flour
butter for filling

Variations

Sweet Potato Cakes
Sprinkle the butter with caster sugar before closing the cakes.

Apple Potato Cakes
Fill with chopped apple, sugar and butter before closing the cakes.

Step 1 Boil, dry and mash the potatoes in a mouli. While still hot, beat in the butter. Season well with salt and freshly ground pepper. Work in sufficient flour to bind into a dough.

Step 2 On a floured board, knead the dough lightly and divide it in half. Shape each piece into a round 1 cm/½ inch thick. Cut each round into 6 or 8 farls (triangles).

Step 3 Well grease the heated girdle. Lift the farls onto the girdle with a palette knife or a fish slice and cook for about 5 minutes until nicely browned underneath. Turn and cook until golden brown.

Step 4 Split the potato cakes, fill with a slice of butter and serve very hot with grilled sausage or bacon.

Bread Making Yeast

Home-baked bread gives pleasure all round; it fills the house with a scent which is both reviving and soothing. Kneading and baking the dough is uniquely satisfying for the home cook, and the crusty brown loaves are as delicious and wholesome to eat as they are attractive to look at.

Yeast: Fresh yeast is easy to handle if you remember that it is a living organism which grows in warmth but is killed by strong heat. It is obtainable at some small bakeries and delicatessens and most health food shops. If wrapped, it will keep for several days in the refrigerator. Dried yeast, in packets of granules, is readily obtainable and will keep for up to 6 months in a cool dry place. It is concentrated, so you need only 15 g/½ oz dried yeast for each 25 g/1 oz of the fresh, but it will take longer to raise the dough. Fresh yeast is added to flour either by rubbing it in, or blending it with liquid. Blending it with liquid is suitable for all bread recipes. Dried yeast must be reconstituted in some of the water used in the recipe and sweetened with 1 teaspoon sugar to each 300 ml/½ pint water.

Flour: The right type of flour is very important for successful bread making. For white bread you need a 'strong' flour, not the fine pastry flour which lacks gluten; use either wholemeal or wheatmeal for brown bread.

Wholemeal and stoneground flour contain 100% wheatgerm and bran and produce a rather solid loaf unless some white flour is mixed with them. Wheatmeal has 80% bran and makes a loaf which is lighter in colour and texture.

Kneading
This is very important as it strengthens the dough and is essential for a good rise and a light, open texture in the finished loaf. Follow steps 2 and 3 carefully.

Proving
This is rising the dough before it is baked and is done twice, before and after shaping. The slower the rise the better the dough (see step 4 on facing page). For a quick bread, the dough can be risen once only, after shaping (p. 148).

Proving dough and finished White Bread

White Bread   Makes two 450 g/1 lb loaves

METRIC	IMPERIAL
750 g strong white flour	*1½ lb strong white flour*
2 teaspoons salt	*2 teaspoons salt*
15 g lard	*½ oz lard*
15 g fresh yeast OR	*½ oz fresh yeast OR*
1½ teaspoons dried yeast,	*1½ teaspoons dried yeast,*
with 1 teaspoon caster sugar	*with 1 teaspoon caster sugar*
450 ml tepid water	*¾ pint tepid water*

Step 1 Sift the flour and salt into a warmed bowl and rub in the lard. Blend the fresh yeast with the water. If using dried yeast, dissolve the sugar in the water, sprinkle in the yeast and leave until frothing. Make a well in the flour and pour in the yeast liquid all at once. Stir and beat with a wooden spoon until the dough leaves the sides of the bowl.

Step 2 Gather the dough into a ball, turn it onto a floured board and flatten it slightly. Hold the front of the dough with one hand, and with the other pull up the further edge, stretch it and fold it over towards you.

Step 3 Press the folded dough down firmly and, with a punching movement, push it away from you, using the heel of your hand. Give the dough a quarter turn and repeat the stretching, folding and punching – developing a rocking movement – for at least 10 minutes, until the dough is firm and elastic and does not stick to the fingers.

Step 4 Shape the dough into a round and put it into a lightly oiled polythene bag and set it aside to rise until it has doubled its bulk – 45 to 60 minutes in a warm place for a quick rise, 1½ to 2 hours at room temperature, 8 to 12 hours in a cold larder, 12 to 14 hours in a refrigerator. Refrigerated dough must be left for about 1 hour at room temperature before being shaped.

Step 5 Grease two ½ kg/1 lb loaf tins or one 1 kg/2 lb tin. For 2 small loaves divide the risen dough in half. Flatten each piece firmly with the knuckles to knock out any air bubbles, then knead again for 2 to 3 minutes. Stretch each piece of dough into a rectangle with a width equal to the length of the tin. Fold the dough in three or roll it up like a Swiss roll and place it in the tins, with the join underneath and pat into shape to fit the corners.

Step 6 Brush the top of the dough with lightly salted water. Place the tins in the oiled polythene bags and leave in a warm place to 'prove', until the dough rises to the top of the tins and is springy to the touch. Remove the tins from the bags, set them on a baking sheet and brush the dough again with the salted water. Bake in the centre of a preheated oven at 230 °C, 450 °F or gas mark 8, for 30 to 40 minutes, until well risen and golden brown.

When cooked, the loaf shrinks slightly from the sides of the tin and sounds hollow when tapped on the bottom. Turn out and cool on a wire tray.

For an extra crusty finish, return the unmoulded loaves to the oven for a further 5 to 10 minutes.

Dinner Rolls

After the risen dough has been divided in half and 'knocked back' (step 5), shape each half into a round and divide into 6 or 8 equal portions. Roll each portion into a ball on the floured palm of your hands, then press it down on the board and flatten it slightly. Arrange the rounds on a baking tray, allowing room to swell, cover with polythene and leave to prove until doubled in size. Bake in a preheated oven at 230 °C, 450 °F or gas mark 8 for 15 to 20 minutes, until crisp and golden.

Quick Brown Bread

METRIC	IMPERIAL
225g wholemeal flour and 225 g strong white flour	*8 oz wholemeal flour and 8 oz strong white flour*
OR	*OR*
450 g wholemeal flour	*1 lb wholemeal flour*
2 teaspoons salt	*2 teaspoons salt*
2 teaspoons caster sugar	*2 teaspoons caster sugar*
10 g lard	*¼ oz lard*
15 g fresh yeast	*½ oz fresh yeast*
OR	*OR*
2 teaspoons dried yeast	*2 teaspoons dried yeast*
300 ml warm water	*½ pint warm water*
2 tablespoons cracked wheat or sesame seeds	*2 tablespoons cracked wheat or sesame seeds*

Makes two 450 g/1 lb loaves

Sift the flour, salt and sugar into a bowl. Tip any bran left in the sieve into the bowl. Cut up the lard and rub it in with the fingertips. If using fresh yeast, dissolve it in the warm water. If using dried, dissolve 1 teaspoon sugar in 150 ml/¼ pint water, sprinkle the yeast on top, leave until frothing and add to the flour with the remaining water. Make a well in the flour and pour in the yeast liquid. Mix to a soft dough and beat with a wooden spoon until it leaves the sides of the bowl clean. Add a little extra water if too stiff.

Turn onto a floured board and knead well (p. 147). Divide the dough in half and shape each piece into a roll to half-fill two greased 450 g/1 lb loaf tins. Brush the top of the dough with slightly salted water and sprinkle with cracked wheat or sesame seeds. Place the tins in lightly oiled plastic bags, close loosely and leave in a warm place until the dough is doubled in bulk, about 1 hour. Remove the dough from the bags and place on a baking sheet. Bake in the centre of a preheated oven at 230 °C, 450 °F or gas mark 8 for 40 to 45 minutes until well risen and the loaf sounds hollow when the bottom is tapped. Turn out and cool on a wire tray.

Quick Brown Bread; Round Cob Loaf; Soft Brown Rolls; Spiced Fruit Loaves

Variations

Round Cob Loaves

Divide the dough in half, shape each piece into a round and place on a greased baking sheet. Finish tops as for tin loaves, prove until doubled in bulk and bake as for Quick brown bread.

Soft Brown Rolls

Divide the dough and shape as for Dinner rolls (p. 147). Place the rolls 2 cm/¾ inches apart on a baking tray and dust generously with flour. Cover with polythene and leave to prove until doubled in bulk. Bake just above the centre of a preheated oven at 230 °C, 450 °F or gas mark 8 for 20 to 30 minutes. The rolls will spread against each other but are easily separated and will have a soft surface instead of a crust.

Spiced Fruit Loaf

METRIC	IMPERIAL
225 g wholemeal flour	8 oz wholemeal flour
225 g strong white flour	8 oz strong white flour
2 teaspoons salt	2 teaspoons salt
1 teaspoon mixed spice	1 teaspoon mixed spice
50 g caster sugar	2 oz caster sugar
10 g lard	¼ oz lard
100 g dried apricots	4 oz dried apricots
50 g chopped walnuts (optional)	2 oz chopped walnuts (optional)
100 g sultanas	4 oz sultanas
50 g seedless raisins	2 oz seedless raisins
15 g fresh yeast	½ oz fresh yeast
OR	OR
2 teaspoons dried yeast	2 teaspoons dried yeast
300 ml warm water	½ pint warm water
TOPPING	TOPPING
25 g butter or margarine	1 oz butter or margarine
25 g caster sugar	1 oz caster sugar
40 g plain flour	1½ oz plain flour

Sift flour, salt, mixed spice and sugar into a large bowl. Tip any bran left in the sieve into the bowl. Rub in the fat. Snip up the apricots with scissors and mix into the flour with the walnuts, sultanas and raisins. Dissolve the yeast in the warm water and make up the dough as for Quick brown bread (on facing page), and knead well. Line the base of 2 greased 450 g/1 lb loaf tins with a strip of non-stick parchment or buttered greaseproof paper. Divide dough in half, shape each piece into a roll and place in the tins. Put into polythene bags, leave in a warm place for about 1 hour or until doubled in bulk. Make the topping by rubbing together the butter, sugar and flour to a rough breadcrumb consistency. Cover the dough evenly with the mixture. Bake in the centre of a preheated oven at 200 °C, 400 °F or gas mark 6 for 40-45 minutes. Allow to shrink for 10 minutes then turn out onto a wire tray to cool.

Some Basics

Filleting fish

Fish weighing 500g (1¼lb) or more are filleted into four, each fillet weighing 75-100g (3-4 oz).

Flat fish: Plaice, Sole etc

Step 1 Lay the cleaned fish on a board, the tail towards you, and cut down the centre on the backbone from head to tail. Insert a thin sharp knife between the flesh and the bone on the left of the backbone, and with slanting strokes, ease the flesh off the bones, working down to the tail. Turn the fish round with the head towards you and remove the other fillets in the same way.

Step 2 Turn the fish over and remove the remaining two fillets in a similar fashion. Trim the fillets neatly and wash under cold running water. Use the head, bones and skin to make fish stock (p. 18).

Step 3 Small flat fish are cut into two 'all over' fillets. Lay the fish on a board, tail towards you, and make a semi-circular cut below the head. Insert the knife between the flesh and the backbone and, working downwards, ease the flesh off in one wide fillet. Turn fish over and remove second fillet.

Round fish: Mackerel, Herring, Whiting etc

Step 1 Cut off the head (excepting trout) and trim off the fins with kitchen scissors. Slit the cleaned fish down the belly and open it out.

Step 2 Spread it out flat, skin side uppermost, on a board and press down firmly along the backbone to loosen it.

Step 3 Turn the fish over and with a pointed knife ease off the backbone, working from the head downwards, and lift it off with the tail. Remove any other small bones and cut the fish down the centre into two fillets.

Large fish: Haddock, Cod, etc

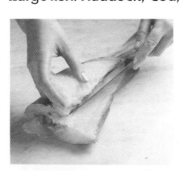

Step 1 Slit down the back instead of the belly, and ease the top fillet off the backbone with the slanted knife.

Step 2 Open the fish out flat and cut off the fillet at the tail. With a pointed knife, ease the backbone off the other fillet and remove with the tail. If the two fillets are very large, each one can be cut diagonally in half to make conveniently sized portions.

To line a cake tin

Cut a double strip of greaseproof paper or non-stick parchment long enough to reach round the inside of the tin and overlap by 4-5 cm/1½-2 inches and wide enough to extend 2.5 cm/1 inch above the top of the tin. Fold up the bottom edge of the strip and crease it firmly. With scissors snip all along the folded strip from its edge up to the crease. Stand the tin on a doubled sheet of greaseproof paper or parchment, draw a circle round it, and cut out 2 rounds.

Brush the inside of the cake tin lightly with oil and line the sides with the strip, fitting the snipped edge flat onto the base. Put in the rounds, which will hold down the snipped edging. Brush the lining with oil or melted fat if using greaseproof paper. This is not necessary with the non-stick parchment.

Separating eggs

It is often necessary to separate the yolk and the white of an egg as only one or the other is needed for a recipe.

It is not serious if a little white remains with the yolk, but if ever a speck of yolk mixes with the white it will be impossible to whisk it into a stiff foam, as the yolk is fatty. Use absolutely clean bowls as even a drop of fat or water will prevent the white whisking up properly.

If you do find a speck of yolk in the white you can sometimes scoop it out with the empty egg shell. The yolk is drawn naturally into the egg shell, but it will be repelled by a spoon and you will chase it in vain.

When separating more than one egg, do not break the second egg over the white of the first one in case you have an accident and broken yolk gets into the white. Separate each egg individually and add yolk to yolks and white to whites.

Step 1 Hold the egg lengthwise in your left hand (if right-handed) and tap smartly in the middle with the back of a knife. This will make a clean crack and not shatter the shell as sometimes happens if you hit the egg on the edge of a thick bowl.

Step 2 Turn the pointed end of the egg upwards so the yolk, which is heavy, will sink into the larger rounded end. Carefully pull off the top half of the shell and allow the white to run down the outside of the bottom shell into a clean bowl.

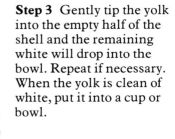

Step 3 Gently tip the yolk into the empty half of the shell and the remaining white will drop into the bowl. Repeat if necessary. When the yolk is clean of white, put it into a cup or bowl.

Bouquet Garni

A small bunch of fresh herbs tied together, or dried herbs tied in a muslin bag, used for flavouring stocks, soups, sauces and casserole dishes. It is left to infuse, i.e. to steep in the cooking liquid to extract the flavour and then removed and discarded. Use a piece of string long enough to tie one end round the handle of the pan so it can easily be withdrawn when required. The basic mixture is a bay leaf, 2 or 3 sprigs of parsley (stalk and leaves) and thyme, but this can be varied or extended with a piece of celery stalk, a sprig of rosemary or marjoram, a crushed clove of garlic or a slice of orange or lemon rind.

Beurre Manié

Kneaded butter and flour used to thicken soups, sauces and casseroles. Mash 2 tablespoons butter with 2 tablespoons flour, using a fork; add a teaspoonful at a time to a gently simmering soup, sauce or casserole until thickened to desired consistency.

Do not boil hard or the sauce will separate, but cook long enough to remove the starchy taste of raw flour. Surplus beurre manié can be closely wrapped and stored in a refrigerator or freezer.

Clarified Butter

Sediment-free butter used for shallow frying.

Step 1 Heat unsalted butter gently until foaming, but do not allow it to brown.

Step 2 Remove the pan from the heat and allow the sediment to settle. Strain the butter through a fine nylon sieve or muslin.

Step 3 Leave it until cold, then lift the solid fat off the liquid.

Croûtons

Fried diced bread served hot with soup or as a filling for Savoury omelettes (p. 34). Slice bread 1cm/½inch thick. Remove the crusts and cut the bread into dice. Deep fry in hot oil (p.66) or shallow fry in butter until golden. Drain on soft paper. Serve at once or store in an airtight container or freezer.

Garlic Butter

Garlic-flavoured butter used for spreading on hot French bread, for grilling meat or flavouring vegetables. Press or chop finely 2 to 4 cloves of garlic and beat into 4 tablespoons creamed butter. Season to taste with salt and freshly ground pepper.

Parsley Butter

Parsley-flavoured butter used for grilling fish or meat or flavouring cooked vegetables.

Beat 1 tablespoon finely chopped parsley into every 2 tablespoons creamed butter. Season with salt and sharpen to taste with lemon juice. Roll into a sausage shape, wrap and chill. Slice and use as a garnish or for cooking.

Index

154

Photography by:

Bryce Attwell: Endpapers, Pages
4-7, 10-13, 18-23, 28-29, 32-35,
38-41, 46-55, 60-61, 68-69, 86-87
(2) (3) (4) (5) (6), 104-105, 116 (1),
134-153.
Melvin Grey: Pages 26-27, 30-31,
42-43, 58-59, 62-67, 70-73, 82-85,
88-103, 106-115, 118-119, 122-133.
Paul Kemp: Pages 14-17, 24-25,
36-37, 44-45, 56-57, 74-81, 86-87 &
(1), 116-117, 120-121.

The publishers would like to thank
the following companies for the
loan of accessories for the
photography in this book:

Advance Domestic Appliances
(Scholtés gas hob)
17 Berners Street,
London, W.1.

Craftsmen Potters Association,
Marshall Street,
London, W.1.

Divertimenti,
68 Marylebone Lane,
London, W.1.

David Mellor, Ironmonger,
4 Sloane Square,
London, SW1.

Elizabeth David,
46 Bourne Street,
London, SW1.

Mappin & Webb, (cutlery)
Regent Street,
London, W.1.

The Conran Shop,
77-79 Fulham Road,
London, SW3.

Trade Unlimited, (pine furniture)
51 Fulham High Street,
London, SW6.

Wedgwood,
Wigmore Street,
London, W.1.

World's End Tiles,
9 Langton Street,
London, SW10.